SPARK

100 DEVOTIONS
TO IGNITE YOUR IMAGINATION

written by Rhonda VanCleave

Nashville TN

T0015669

Published by B&H Publishing Group,
Nashville, Tennessee

Dewey Decimal Classification: C242.62
Subject Heading: DEVOTIONAL LEADERSHIP / IMAGINATION / CREATIVITY

1 2 3 4 5 6 7 • 26 25 24 23 22

CONTENTS

GOD, THE CREATOR

GOD, THE DESIGNER

JESUS, THE KING

JESUS, THE REDEEMER

HOLY SPIRIT, THE HELPER

IN THE BEGINNING

**In the beginning God created the
heavens and the earth.** *Genesis 1:1*

Micah stared at the computer screen. He typed a word or two, then deleted everything. *How do I get started writing this paper?* he thought to himself. The assignment was to write one hundred words about any subject. *How do you start from nothing?* he wondered. Micah thought about his Bible reading that morning from Genesis 1. *Wow, God,* he thought. *You really started with nothing. Then You created the most amazing world!*

As Micah thought more about the things he had read, he realized that God had ordered the days of creation with a plan and a purpose. For example, before something was created, the things it needed to exist were created first. Water was created before fish were placed in it. Land came first, then plants. Food grew before animals needed to eat it. Suddenly Micah knew exactly what he would write about. He would write about God's amazing world. His fingers flew across the keyboard as he began to type, "In the beginning God . . ."

Choose one of the following creative sparks to do today.

1. Draw a sketch of some of your favorite parts of God's creation.

2. Write a prayer telling God about your favorite parts of His creation.

PRAY

God, You are the amazing Creator. Today I want to
thank You for Your creation. *(Read your prayer aloud
to God or thank Him for the item you sketched.)*

2

VERY GOOD INDEED

God saw all that he had made, and it was very good indeed. Evening came and then morning: the sixth day. *Genesis 1:31*

With His words, God spoke the land, sea, sky, sun, moon, stars, plants, trees, birds, fish, and animals into existence. Then, on the sixth day, God personally formed the man and the woman, breathing the breath of life into them. God looked at His creation and declared that "it was very good indeed."

People are a special part of creation for God. This means you are part of God's special creation. It means you are also part of what God considers "very good indeed." God knows you. He planned for you and for each day of your life. He knows you will make mistakes and even wrong choices sometimes, but He loves you because He created you. God loves you on your best days and your worst days. That's something to feel very good about.

TODAY'S SPARK

Choose one of the following creative sparks to do today.

1. Draw a self-portrait below. Look in a mirror and sketch what you look like.

2. Make a list of things you know about yourself, such as "brown eyes, love my dog, like to listen to music, enjoy reading." Include things you both like and don't like about yourself.

PRAY

God, sometimes I don't feel good about myself
because I forget that You created me and love me.
*(Continue talking with God about the things you drew or
listed. Ask Him to help you remember that He is your Creator.)*

3

IN THE LIKENESS OF GOD

This is the document containing the family records of Adam. On the day that God created man, he made him in the likeness of God; he created them male and female. When they were created, he blessed them and called them mankind. *Genesis 5:1–2*

What makes human beings different from all other parts of creation? My dog knows how to comfort me when I'm sad. The squirrels seem really smart because they can get food out of the bird feeders—even when we use the ones that say squirrels can't get at the food!

Still, my dog and the squirrels are not like us. God said that people are made "in the likeness of God." That means God has given us a special place in creation to work with Him to care for creation. We are also created to have a relationship with God as our heavenly Father. Because of this, we can reason and think. We can be creative. We can make choices, which means we can choose to love and obey God, or we can choose not to. Which choice do you want to make?

TODAY'S SPARK

Choose one of the following creative sparks to do today.

1. Do you like to act? Practice reading today's verses (Genesis 5:1–2) as if you were reading a declaration from a king. (You are! It is a declaration from God!)

2. If you have some clay or play dough, make a ball, then press your thumb deep into the ball. Compare the clay image of your thumb with your real thumb. You can tell your thumb made the imprint because you see the image. Think about how God sees the image of Himself when He looks at you.

PRAY

God, being made in Your image or likeness is hard to understand. I know I don't "look" like You, but You help me see the world like You do. *(Ask God to help you continue to learn what it means to be "made in His likeness.")*

4

THE WONDER OF CREATION

You, Lord, are the only God. You created the heavens, the highest heavens with all their stars, the earth and all that is on it, the seas and all that is in them. You give life to all of them, and all the stars of heaven worship you. *Nehemiah 9:6*

Jakena and her mom were taking a walk through the park. They were talking about the many things in God's creation that they were enjoying. The wind was ruffling the leaves of the trees. The flowers were in full bloom. Birds were singing. A funny chipmunk startled them as he darted across their path. "Mom," Jakena said, "Sometimes I feel closer to God when I'm outside enjoying nature."

"Me too," Mom replied. "I think that's partly because of all the living things we see that God made. We can read about creation in Genesis. But did you know that many other Bible writers celebrated God and His amazing creation too?"

"Really?" Jakena asked. "Can we read some of them?"

"Sure!" Mom replied. "I'll make a list, and we can read a verse each morning at breakfast."

"Great idea!" Jakena exclaimed.

TODAY'S SPARK

Choose one of the following creative sparks to do today.

1. Create a list of Bible verses that celebrate God's creation. You can begin with today's verse, Nehemiah 9:6. Here are some others to consider: Psalm 104:24, Isaiah 40:28, Psalm 96:11–12, Psalm 95:4–5, Psalm 33:6, and Jeremiah 10:12.

2. Sketch some leaf shapes or place a leaf under this page and create a rubbing with a crayon or colored pencil. Think about the details God put into just a leaf.

PRAY

God, Your creation is amazing! Thank You for giving us so much to enjoy in nature. *(Talk to God about some details you notice like the colors on tree bark, the veins of the leaf, or the parts of a flower.)*

5

GOD MADE THE STARS

He makes the stars: the Bear, Orion, the Pleiades,
and the constellations of the southern sky. He does great and
unsearchable things, wonders without number. *Job 9:9–10*

Uncle Billy used to work for NASA," Noah declared.

"Really?" asked his friend Sam.

"Yep, and he has a huge telescope in his backyard in a special shed with a roof that slides open!"

"No way!" Sam said. "Does he ever let you look through it?"

"I'm going over tonight. You can come too if you want."

Later that evening, the boys arrived at Uncle Billy's. When he pushed a button and the shed roof slid off onto a platform, they were amazed. Uncle Billy adjusted some knobs on the telescope and let the boys take a look. He stated the names of some of the stars and constellations.

"Did you name all those stars?" Sam asked in awe.

Uncle Billy chuckled. "No. Sometimes we discover a new star we haven't seen before and someone will give it a name. But did you know that in one of the oldest books of the Bible, Job, you can read the names of some of the stars and constellations? God made them, and He knows all about them!"

TODAY'S SPARK

Choose one of the following creative sparks to do today.

1. In the dot-to-dot below, start with Polaris (the North Star), then connect the stars to outline the Little Dipper. Next connect the stars to outline the Big Dipper. Both of these star patterns are parts of larger constellations.

2. Look up information about the North Star to discover why it has been important for hundreds of years. Jot down a few facts that you find.

PRAY

God, You created the North Star and put it in
its place. After all this time, it is still there!
*(Worship God for knowing every star in the
universe. Then read about that in Psalm 147:4.)*

6

GOD MADE THE SEASONS

You set all the boundaries of the earth; you made summer and winter. *Psalm 74:17*

Some people live where winters are cold and summers are hot. Some live where it is cold year-round or hot year-round. No matter where you live, there are seasons. This means there are times when things are planted, and there are times when things are harvested. There are growing times and times when things don't grow as much. God's plan from the very beginning was for everything to exist and thrive in its place. Even our earth has a special place in our solar system as it travels around the sun; our planet follows the pattern God set for it from the beginning.

God made the world, and He is still in complete control over it. Some people use the word *sovereign* to describe how God is ultimately in control. The things God made—the sun, moon, stars, and seasons—still follow the plan He designed for them. God has plans for us too. He knew we'd be living right now in this place (Acts 17:26).

TODAY'S SPARK

Choose one of the following creative sparks to do today.

1. Make a four-square grid in the space below, and draw a picture in each square of what different seasons look like where you live.

2. Write a short paragraph about your favorite season and why you like it.

PRAY

God, thank You for creating boundaries in our world. Thank You that I live right here, where You placed me. *(Talk to God about some of the things you like about the seasons where you live.)*

7

GOD IS OUR SHEPHERD

Acknowledge that the Lord is God. He made us, and we are his—his people, the sheep of his pasture. *Psalm 100:3*

Kathryn finished her paper for school and printed out a clean copy. "Dad, would you read my report and tell me what you think before I turn it in?" she asked her dad.

"Sure," Dad said as he began to read. "This is really interesting. Looks like you've learned a lot about taking care of sheep."

"Yeah, I was *not* excited about my assignment until I began to do some research. I found out sheep are kinda dumb. And they can even die if the shepherd doesn't look out for them *all the time*."

"Did you think about how often the Bible calls us God's sheep and talks about how we belong in His pasture?" Dad asked. "People in Bible times took care of lots of sheep, and they understood exactly what it meant to be part of God's flock. Sheep need to know their shepherd, and we need to know who our God is."

"Oh, I get it!" Kathryn exclaimed. "It's best when the sheep follow the shepherd's voice, just like it's best when we follow God."

TODAY'S SPARK

Choose one of the following creative sparks to do today.

1. Use some chenille stems or other craft items to make a sheep. Look at your sheep as a reminder that we are part of God's flock, and it is best when we listen to Him.

2. Paint today's verse on a large sheet of paper, and draw images of sheep and pastures around it.

PRAY

God, thank You for being my Good Shepherd.
I can trust You. *(Thank God for the many ways
He cares for you. Tell Him you want to follow Him
because you trust where He will lead you.)*

8

"HOW COUNTLESS ARE YOUR WORKS, LORD!"

How countless are your works, Lord! In wisdom you have made them all; the earth is full of your creatures. *Psalm 104:24*

Can you count the grains of sand on the beach? Or every snowflake that falls? What about all the stars in the sky? Even if we could count all those things, think about the things we can't see to count, like sound waves, atoms, and skin cells!

God thought of all the details in everything that exists. He made your fingerprints unique to you. He knows how many hairs are on your head (Luke 12:7). When we think about how "countless" (that means "too many to count") are the works of our God, we are amazed. And when we think about the teeny, tiny details God included, like how our hearts and lungs work, we realize how awesome our God is. We often pray to God to ask Him to help people we care about or to provide something we need. But have you ever prayed to God praising and thanking Him for His amazing, detailed creation?

TODAY'S SPARK

Choose one of the following creative sparks to do today.

1. Make a list of other things that are "too many to count," like blades of grass or leaves in a forest. Can you think of ten more?

2. Have you learned a song recently with today's Bible verse in it? If you have, can you sing it? If not, try turning the verse into a song by creating your own melody and rhythm.

PRAY

God, thank You that You know the details of all Your creation, even details about me that I don't know! *(Read today's Bible verse as a prayer. Then thank God for all the details He included in creation.)*

9

OUR POWERFUL GOD

There the ships move about, and Leviathan, which you formed to play there. *Psalm 104:26*

"Nana," Emma asked after she returned from church, "What is *la-VI-a-than*?"

"Leviathan?" Nana replied. "Well, you can find it mentioned a few places in the Bible. We're not sure. It may even be extinct now. But according to the book of Job, it was a massive sea creature."

"Was it big like an elephant or a whale?" Emma asked.

"It may have been much larger. God told Job it was so big, no person would dare fight with it. God was helping Job understand that God is more powerful than even the most powerful sea creature humans knew about at the time."

"Oh, wow!" Emma exclaimed. "Where can I read about that?"

"Job chapter 41," Nana said. "I'll go get my Bible, and we can read it together."

As Nana walked away, Emma thought about how God created everything, even leviathan, so He must be pretty powerful.

TODAY'S SPARK

Choose one of the following creative sparks to do today.

1. Read Job 41 and draw what you think leviathan might have looked like.

2. Use a Bible app or concordance to look up Bible passages that talk about leviathan. Write a short report.

PRAY

God, some things You created are huge and can be scary.
Help me remember You are more powerful than
they are because You created them. *(Talk to God about
what scares you, and remember He can take care of you.)*

10

GOD HAS ALWAYS BEEN HERE

Look up and see! Who created these? He brings out the stars by number; he calls all of them by name. Because of his great power and strength, not one of them is missing. Isaiah 40:26

Our family uses an app on our tablets that helps us know what we are seeing in the night sky. We can identify planets and stars. We can find constellations and moons. We can sometimes track satellites or the International Space Station. It's amazing how technology helps us identify things so far away!

Hundreds of years ago, people used those same stars to navigate across the ocean or travel through wildernesses. The very same stars our family will look at tonight are the ones our grandparents saw, early settlers saw, people in Jesus' time saw, and people in Isaiah's time saw. What an amazing thought to realize that we are looking at the same stars written about in the Bible! It makes me think, *Wow, God! You made those stars that have lasted for so long! You are the same God Isaiah worshiped, people in the New Testament worshiped, my grandparents worshiped, and our family worships. You have always existed!*

TODAY'S SPARK

Choose one of the following creative sparks to do today.

1. Write a letter to a friend who lives far away. Let them know you think about them when you look at the stars that both of you can see.

2. Draw a picture of something that has been on earth for a very long time, like a mountain or a waterfall. While you draw, remember that God created it, and God has always been here.

PRAY

God, the Bible reminds me that You created the stars. You were here before they existed! *(Tell God how you feel when Hebrews 13:8 reminds you He is "the same yesterday, today, and forever.")*

11

GOD IS AMAZING

Do you not know? Have you not heard? The Lord is the everlasting God, the Creator of the whole earth. He never becomes faint or weary; there is no limit to his understanding. *Isaiah 40:28*

Andre helped Uncle Jim carry the last load out of the shed and toss it in the dumpster. "There was so much stuff in that shed. I'm exhausted *and* hungry!" Andre exclaimed.

Uncle Jim gave Andre a pat on the back. "We did good work today. I think it's time for an extra-large pizza."

"All right!" Andre cheered.

Later, as the two munched away on a pizza, Andre asked, "Do you think God ever gets tired? I mean, He does keep up with everything that's happening everywhere all the time. That sounds exhausting."

"There's one big difference between humans and God," Uncle Jim explained. "We have limits. God included that when He designed the world. He gave us nighttime to rest, and He gave nature the different seasons to rest. But the Bible tells us that God never gets tired. He is all-powerful, and He is all-knowing."

TODAY'S SPARK

Choose one of the following creative sparks to do today.

1. Make a list of things you'd like to do this week, and check them off as you do them. Be sure to include time with God on your list. At the end of the week, if you didn't get through everything, remember that humans have limits, unlike God. Praise God for His limitless nature.

2. Sometimes doing chores is easier when you add music. Can you make up a song to sing while you are completing a chore? Or is there a favorite song you might play in the background?

PRAY

God, You are amazing! The Bible says that there is no limit to Your strength or understanding.
(Ask God to give you the strength to do something you know will take a lot of energy.)

12

A WORLD TO ENJOY

This is what the LORD says—the Creator of the heavens, the God who formed the earth and made it, the one who established it (he did not create it to be a wasteland, but formed it to be inhabited)— he says, "I am the LORD, and there is no other." Isaiah 45:18

People live in lots of types of places. Some people have front yards and neighbors up and down the street. Some people live in tall buildings with neighbors up and down the hall. Some people live in homes surrounded by nature, with neighbors who are miles away. But they all have one thing in common. They live in the world God created.

Today's verse reminds us that God didn't create the world to be a vast wasteland. He created it for us to live here and enjoy what He has created. Look around where you live. What parts of God's creation can you see? You might see a plant in your house or a field full of plants across the road. You might see birds or bugs or a bright blue sky. When you look at the things God made, remember that He is the Creator. He established this world, and He made it for us to enjoy.

TODAY'S SPARK

Choose one of the following creative sparks to do today.

1. Did you know that some neighborhoods were planned by professional designers? Draw a map of an imaginary neighborhood you would like to live in. Would you include fun areas like playgrounds or swimming pools? Would the houses have big yards or small ones?

2. Keep a journal for a week, listing what you see out your window that's part of God's creation (clouds, leaves, birds, and so on). If you know the terms, be specific (e.g., cardinals, blue jays, or doves).

PRAY

God, You made the world for us to live in. Thank You for so many wonderful things to see and enjoy! *(Thank God for what you can see, hear, taste, touch, or smell right now.)*

13

GOD KEEPS EVERYTHING GOING

The one who made the Pleiades and Orion, who turns darkness into dawn and darkens day into night, who summons the water of the sea and pours it out over the surface of the earth—the LORD is his name. *Amos 5:8*

Have you ever noticed how many times the authors of the Bible remind us that God is the great Creator? Today's verse is from Amos, a book you can find in the Old Testament. It is one of the shorter books of a section of Scripture called *Prophecy*.

Amos reminded the people that God is great: He created all the stars in the skies that make up constellations like Pleiades and Orion, and He keeps them in their places. Amos pointed out that God keeps the world spinning, which gives us daytime and nighttime. God created the evaporation cycle so we could receive rain to help plants grow. God made everything, and His perfect plan keeps everything going!

What other patterns in nature do you see? Worship God for creating and establishing them.

TODAY'S SPARK

Choose one of the following creative sparks to do today.

1. All of God's Word, the Bible, is important. Start keeping a list of the books of the Bible you have read verses from and include one thing you learned from that verse. Start with today's book, Amos.

2. Poems sometimes rhyme and sometimes don't. Try writing a poem about the things you see in the sky at night, in the daytime, or both.

PRAY

God, thank You for taking care of the stars, the cycles of the earth, and every one of my days. Help me trust in You.
(Tell God about something you need His help with today.)

14
FROM THE BEGINNING

In the beginning was the Word, and the Word was with God, and the Word was God. He was with God in the beginning. All things were created through him, and apart from him not one thing was created that has been created. *John 1:1–3*

Victoria was reading her Bible during her quiet time. She decided to read the book of John in the New Testament. She read the first three verses of John, but it seemed stumped. She read it several more times, but she was still stumped. "Mom," she asked, "What *Word* was with God?"

"Just say the name *Jesus* when you see *the Word* in those verses," her mom said. "John was helping people understand that Jesus is God. Jesus was there at the beginning when the world was created," she explained.

Victoria tried that, and suddenly the verse began to make more sense. "I get it now," she told her mom. "Jesus is God. He was there at the Creation, and everything that was created was made by Him!"

TODAY'S SPARK

Choose one of the following creative sparks to do today.

1. Create patterns of different colors to spell the name "Jesus" on a mini poster.

2. Using scraps of paper, create a collage of other names you know that mean Jesus, such as "Word," "Son of God," "Savior," and so on.

PRAY

Jesus, You have always existed. That's hard to understand, but I trust what the Bible says about You is true. *(Thank God for the Bible and how it helps you know about Jesus.)*

15

JESUS IN THE WORLD

He was in the world, and the world was created through him, and yet the world did not recognize him. *John 1:10*

Jesus was with God in the beginning when the world was created. Then, when the time was right, God sent Him to live in the world and to take the punishment for our sins as our Savior. Jesus created the world and came to live in the world, yet most of the people around Him did not realize or recognize who Jesus was!

John was one of Jesus' disciples. John wrote one of the Gospels, or a book of the Bible that tells the good news about what Jesus did when He came to earth. John said that if everything Jesus did were written down, the world could not contain all the books (John 21:25)!

Even though Jesus did countless amazing things, John still wrote, "the world did not recognize Him." That would discourage most of us, but not Jesus. Jesus finished the work He came to do as our Savior.

TODAY'S SPARK

Choose one of the following creative sparks to do today.

1. What are some songs you know about Jesus? Hum the tune while you think about the words, then sing the song as a praise song to Jesus.

2. What are some things you know Jesus did while on earth? What are some things you know He has done for you? Make a list of those things.

PRAY

Thank You, Jesus, for coming to earth to be our Savior. *(Talk to Jesus about some specific things He has done that you are grateful for.)*

16

JESUS, LORD OF CREATION

When they heard this, they raised their voices together to God and said, "Master, you are the one who made the heaven, the earth, and the sea, and everything in them." *Acts 4:24*

For many people, it's easy to praise God when they are enjoying special times or observing God's amazing creation. But, if you read the full story in Acts 4, you will see Peter and John were arrested, held in prison overnight, and ordered to stop preaching about Jesus.

What? Stop telling people about Jesus?

Peter and John understood the ruling, but they said they could never stop talking about what they knew about Jesus. Peter and John had spent time with Jesus and heard the things He taught. How could they stop sharing His wonderful truth?

When they went back to the group of believers and told them what had happened, the people did not panic or act scared. Instead, they praised God (verse 24) because they knew Jesus is the Lord of all creation.

TODAY'S SPARK

Choose one of the following creative sparks to do today.

1. Write a prayer to God, asking Him to help you feel excited to talk about Jesus, even when others don't believe you.

2. Create some word art. Write words you think of when you think about Jesus; then add doodles and decorations to turn your words into art.

PRAY

Thank You, Jesus, for being Lord of creation.
Help me be brave and tell others about You.
(Read the last part of today's verse as a prayer.)

17

LORD OVER ALL

Whatever you do, do it from the heart, as something done for the Lord and not for people. Colossians 3:23

Kyle was trying to finish his math homework. It was not going well. He slammed his pencil down in frustration and exclaimed, "Why do I even have to do this homework? It's not fair that teachers can just tell you what to do. I'll be glad when I grow up and no one can boss me around!"

Mom put the last few groceries away and then said, "You know, Kyle, we all have someone who tells us what to do . . . teachers, bosses, and even the government. In fact, one day *you* may be someone's boss. You may have to tell them to do things they don't want to do. The important thing to remember is that God is Lord over *all* things. If we follow Him, we will be doing the things we are supposed to do for the right reasons."

Kyle thought for a few minutes. "So, for now, I may not like what I'm told to do, but if I am also doing those things to honor God, that changes how I think about it."

Mom nodded, and Kyle picked up his pencil again, determined to do well on his assignment.

TODAY'S SPARK

Choose one of the following creative sparks to do today.

1. Think of one of your favorite teachers. Write them a note, telling them some of the things you love about being in their class.

2. If you could be the boss of something, what would it be? What rules would you make? Draw a picture of something you would like to be in charge of.

PRAY

God, I know You are in control of everything,
even who my teachers, coaches, and parents are.
(Thank God for the adults in your life you enjoy.
Pray for the ones you have a harder time with.)

18

FAITH IN THE CREATOR

By faith we understand that the universe was created by the word of God, so that what is seen was made from things that are not visible. *Hebrews 11:3*

Granddad could tell something was troubling Tim while they were working in the yard. "What's the matter, buddy?" Granddad asked. "I can tell you are seriously thinking about something."

Tim shrugged. "Yesterday, a few of us were talking about how the world began. I know God created it, and I thought everyone else believed the same thing. But, wow, my friends have all kinds of ideas. Now I'm not sure what to believe."

Granddad nodded. "I understand. I've had some of the same questions myself. But I realized that people who choose to believe something other than what the Bible says about God are also trusting in things we can't see. I choose to believe the Bible because it has proven to be true and trustworthy throughout human history. Faith is choosing to believe God, even though we can't see Him. We weren't there when God created everything from nothing, but we know by faith that God has the power to do just that."

TODAY'S SPARK

Choose one of the following creative sparks to do today.

1. Look again at Genesis 1, and make a list of the things God made from nothing. Add pictures to help you remember.

2. Everything we, as humans, make starts from something. Look at the squiggle line below. Begin with that squiggle and draw an image of something fun.

PRAY

God, I believe You are the Creator. I know other people don't believe that, but help me to keep sharing my faith with them. *(Pray for your friends who may still not believe in Jesus.)*

19

PRAISE GOD FOR ALL THINGS

Our Lord and God, you are worthy to receive glory and honor and power, because you have created all things, and by your will they exist and were created. *Revelation 4:11*

From the beginning of the Bible (Genesis) through the last book of the Bible (Revelation), we see that God is the great Creator. As we've looked at Scripture in these devotions, we've read poetry, prophecy, history, and wisdom revealing truths about God and His plan for humankind. Scripture says even in heaven, God is worshiped as the One who created all things and who continues to keep the universe going.

But God did not create us and then hide Himself from us. He has given us many ways to get to know Him: We can read His Word. We can talk to Him in prayer. We can enjoy the world around us He made. We can have community with other believers. And we can praise Him. All these things draw us even closer to our amazing, loving Creator.

TODAY'S SPARK

Choose one of the following creative sparks to do today.

1. Try writing a simple poem praising God as our amazing, loving Creator.

2. Many songs begin as poetry. If you wrote a poem, try thinking up a melody and rhythm to go with it. Or start with the melody: begin to hum and see if that turns into a melody, then think of words that fit it.

PRAY

God, Your Word is filled with verses that praise You as Creator. Thank You for creating me and not hiding Yourself from me. *(Continue to thank God for other things He has created, and tell Him you want to know Him more.)*

20

GOD IS STILL THE CREATOR

"I will create a new heaven and a new earth; the past events will not be remembered or come to mind." *Isaiah 65:17*

The Bible tells us God created a perfect world, then placed the man and the woman in it to look after it and enjoy it with Him. However, sin entered the world and broke that perfect relationship between God and people.

We still enjoy most of the amazing things God created, like trees, birds, animals, fish, and all of nature. However, because of sin, our world is broken. People experience pain, sadness, sickness, and death—sometimes lots of it.

God sent His Son, Jesus, into the world to be our Savior. When we receive God's gift of forgiveness and trust Jesus, our relationship with Him is restored. We have a relationship with God, and He is with us throughout our lives, no matter what is going on!

But that's not the end of the story. God plans to create a new heaven and a new earth. Someday, things will be made right again. And, best of all, those of us who trust in Him will live with Him forever.

TODAY'S SPARK

Choose one of the following creative sparks to do today.

1. Make an acrostic. Print the word *CREATOR* vertically on a sheet of paper, then add a word that describes God or His creation horizontally beside each letter.

2. Go on a nature walk and collect a few items to use to make a nature collage. At home, glue them to a sheet of construction paper.

PRAY

God, it is exciting to look back on all You've done for me and all You're going to do in the future because of Jesus. Thank You! *(If you haven't trusted in Jesus as your Savior, ask God to help you understand what that means.)*

21

WE ARE GOD'S DESIGN

It was you who created my inward parts; you knit me together in my mother's womb. Psalm 139:13

Natalie was excited about becoming a big sister. She helped her mom get the nursery ready, and her mom let her pick out a couple of toys for her new sister.

One day, Mom came back from her doctor visit with something special to show Natalie. It was a 3-D ultrasound picture of Natalie's baby sister, who would join their family in just a few weeks. Natalie looked in amazement at the chubby cheeks, the little nose, and the tiny mouth curved into a smile. "She looks so cute," Natalie said to her mom. "I knew she was growing inside you, but I didn't know she would already look like a baby."

Mom smiled. "It is amazing how God chose to make all of us. He carefully creates us and helps us develop before we are even born. Each human is God's own special design."

TODAY'S SPARK

Choose one of the following creative sparks to do today.

1. Create a scrapbook page about the day you were born or the day you joined your family. Include the date and any other facts about that special day.

2. Decorate a paper gift bag to give to a new mom. You can make a baby foot by making a fist and pressing the outside of your fist onto an ink pad, then onto the gift bag. (This is the main part of the foot.) To make tiny toes, press your fingerprints onto the ink pad and then onto the paper, along the top of the foot.

PRAY

God, You were with me, helping me grow, even before I was born. Thank You for caring for me since the very beginning. *(Thank God for the life and family He has given you.)*

22

GOD'S DESIGN FOR DAVID

The Lᴏʀᴅ said to Samuel, "Do not look at his appearance or his stature because I have rejected him. Humans do not see what the Lᴏʀᴅ sees, for humans see what is visible, but the Lᴏʀᴅ sees the heart." *1 Samuel 16:7*

King David did not grow up in a palace. He was a shepherd boy. He loved music and could play the lyre, which is a type of harp. David also wrote poems, many of which you can find in the Bible.

When David was still a boy, God told the prophet Samuel to go to Bethlehem to anoint the next king. There, Samuel met with a man named Jesse who had seven sons. When Samuel saw the oldest son, Samuel thought he was the perfect choice for a king! But God said no. God also said no to five of the other sons.

When Samuel heard that Jesse's youngest son was still in the fields with the sheep, they sent for him. As soon as David arrived, God let Samuel know He had chosen David— not because of what he looked like on the outside, but because of his heart. David loved God deeply.

It would be years before David would reign as king. David had to be patient. But God used those years to prepare David to rule over Israel.

TODAY'S SPARK

Choose one of the following creative sparks to do today.

1. Do you like to read stories about people? Read 1 Samuel 16 to find out more about this event in David's life.

2. David enjoyed music. Do you play an instrument? If you do, try playing a praise song to God. That's something David often did.

PRAY

God, You had a special design for David's life, and You made it happen. Then David had to trust You and be patient. *(Ask God to help you follow His design for your life.)*

23

GOD'S DESIGN FOR ESTHER

Perhaps you have come to your royal position for such a time as this. *Esther 4:14*

The story of Esther is found in the Old Testament. Have you heard it before? Esther didn't have the easiest life. For example, Esther's parents died when she was young. Thankfully, her cousin Mordecai took her into his family and raised her like a daughter. She knew she was loved and cared for.

Later, when the king sent out an order for young women to be brought to the palace, Esther was chosen. Eventually Esther was selected as queen! But during her reign, an evil, powerful man named Haman planned to have all the Jews destroyed. Esther was Jewish, but neither the king nor Haman knew it. Esther went before the king to plead for her people. She was afraid because she didn't know how the king would respond. But her cousin Mordecai said maybe this was why God had made her queen.

God had a plan, and Esther was brave enough to follow God's plan. You can read the whole story in the book of the Bible named (you guessed it!) Esther.

TODAY'S SPARK

Choose one of the following creative sparks to do today.

1. Kings and queens often wear crowns. Design a crown you would like to wear. You can draw one or make one using craft supplies.

2. What are some ways God has used you to help others because of your circumstances? Write about a time you helped someone or showed up just when you were needed. If you want, add illustrations.

PRAY

God, give me the courage to do what You have designed for me to do. *(Ask God to show you the things He wants you to do because of where you live, the people you know, and the gifts you have.)*

24

GOD'S DESIGN FOR JEREMIAH

I chose you before I formed you in the womb; I set you apart before you were born. I appointed you a prophet to the nations. *Jeremiah 1:5*

Jeremiah was young when God told him he would become a prophet. In fact, Jeremiah said, "Oh no, Lord God! Look, I don't know how to speak since I am only a youth" (Jeremiah 1:6). Jeremiah was worried he didn't have enough knowledge or experience, but God had set him apart as a prophet long before he was born. God promised to protect Jeremiah and to give him the words to say. (A true prophet of God only tells people the messages God gives him or her to share.)

God chose Jeremiah and knew Jeremiah would follow God's instructions. Jeremiah often had to share bad news with the people because they had disobeyed God. Jeremiah's job was not easy! But Jeremiah followed God's design for his life when he was obedient to give God's messages to the people.

TODAY'S SPARK

Choose one of the following creative sparks to do today.

1. Draw a stick figure or outline of a person. On the left side, list things kids typically can do. On the right side, list things that are difficult for kids to do because of their age. Remember Jeremiah was worried he didn't have enough knowledge or experience? But God had a plan for his life—and yours!

2. Find instructions online for an art project. Follow the instructions step by step, word by word. Remember that, as a prophet, Jeremiah paid close attention to God's words.

PRAY

God, Your design for me was Your plan even before I was born. I understand that it might not always be easy, but I want to follow Your will for my life. *(Ask God to help you obey Him, both now and when you grow up.)*

25

GOD'S DESIGN FOR JOHN THE BAPTIST

You, child, will be called a prophet of the Most High, for you will go before the Lord to prepare his ways. Luke 1:76

The Old Testament is filled with prophecies about God's plan to send His Son to be our Savior. It also talks about God sending someone to let people know that Jesus was coming! That person's name was John.

When John was born, his father, Zechariah, prophesied that his child would prepare the way for the Lord's coming. When John grew up, he did exactly that. He preached in wilderness places, and crowds of people came to hear him. Many repented and were baptized to show that they were sorry for their sins and wanted to follow God. When the time was right, John declared Jesus was "the Lamb of God, who takes away the sin of the world" (John 1:29).

Because John baptized people who chose to follow God, he became known as John the Baptizer, or as we know him, John the Baptist.

TODAY'S SPARK

Choose one of the following creative sparks to do today.

1. Read Mark 1:1–6. Draw a picture of what you think John the Baptist might have looked like.

2. Write a haiku poem about John the Baptist. A haiku poem is three lines long. The first line has five syllables. The second line has seven syllables. The third line has five syllables.

PRAY

God, You had a plan for John the Baptist's life,
and it came true. I can always trust Your words.
*(Thank God for people like John the Baptist, who followed
God's plan and helped people know about Jesus.)*

26

GOD'S DESIGN FOR PAUL

God, who from my mother's womb set me apart and called me by his grace, was pleased to reveal his Son in me, so that I could preach him among the Gentiles. *Galatians 1:15–16*

Paul was a grown man before he discovered God's design for his life. He thought he was doing everything right. He had studied the Scriptures, he was an important person, and he tried to carefully keep the Jewish law. But Paul was missing an important part of the truth: He did not understand that Jesus was the *Messiah*, or God's Son and promised Savior.

One day, Paul was traveling to a town called Damascus to arrest some followers of Jesus when he had an experience that left him blind temporarily but changed forever. Paul saw a bright light and heard the voice of Jesus! Jesus told Paul that God had chosen him to take the good news of salvation to the *Gentiles*, or people who weren't Jews. As a Jew, this was shocking to Paul, but he did it anyway.

Several years later, Paul wrote to a church in Galatia. He told them that he knew this had been God's plan for his life since before he was born.

TODAY'S SPARK

Choose one of the following creative sparks to do today.

1. Read Acts 9:1–20. Next, write the story to share with a younger friend or sibling by using simpler words to help them understand.

2. A storyboard is a series of pictures that show the events in a story. Read Acts 9:1–20 and create a storyboard of four or five important scenes in the story.

PRAY

God, I know You have a design for my life.
Thank You that even if I mess up, Your plan for me
is still in the works. *(Ask God to guide you in both big and
small decisions as you do your best to follow Him.)*

27

GOD'S DESIGN FOR TIMOTHY

Don't let anyone despise your youth, but set an example for the believers. . . . Don't neglect the gift that is in you. *1 Timothy 4:12, 14*

Most of the time, God's design for you is also part of the design He has planned for another person. For example, God had a plan for Paul to tell others about Jesus. Part of that plan was for Paul to mentor a young pastor named Timothy.

Timothy's mother and grandmother had taught him about God, and he knew quite a lot before he met Paul. But Paul helped Timothy learn even more, including how to pastor some of the new churches Paul had started.

Timothy may have been worried that he couldn't lead a church since he was younger than some of the people who came. But Paul told Timothy not to worry about that; instead, Timothy should set a good example for all the believers. Paul knew God had given Timothy the gifts he needed to do the work God was giving him to do.

TODAY'S SPARK

Choose one of the following creative sparks to do today.

1. Who is someone who has taught you about Jesus? Write them a thank you note for sharing the good news with you.

2. What gifts has God given you to share the good news about Jesus with others? Draw a picture of what it would look like for you to use them.

PRAY

Thank You, God, for the plans You have for me and for all the people who have helped me learn about You. *(Ask God to help you share what you know with other people.)*

28

DESIGNED TO BE CARETAKERS

You made him ruler over the works of your hands; you put everything under his feet. *Psalm 8:6*

Tristan counted his money carefully. He had enough! He had finally saved enough for a dog. He could pay the adoption fee and buy the supplies his dad said he needed. Tristan's dad said they could go on Saturday to buy the supplies and meet his new dog.

"I know you are excited about getting a dog," Dad said. "But I want you to realize something very important. God gave people the responsibility of helping take care of the things He created. When you get a pet, you are agreeing to partner with God to take care of the animal. Your dog will depend on you for food, water, and exercise outside."

"I'm excited about taking care of my dog, but I didn't think about it being something God designed for people to do," Tristan said thoughtfully. "That makes it feel even more special."

TODAY'S SPARK

Choose one of the following creative sparks to do today.

1. Use ten words only to describe your pet or a pet you would like to have. Try to choose the most precise words possible. If you want, draw this pet as well.

2. Make a one-week calendar on a piece of paper. List what supplies you need to take care of your pet each day.

PRAY

God, our pets are gifts from You. Help me remember that I honor You when I take care of the animals You have made. *(If you don't have a pet, ask God to help you think of other ways to help take care of His creation.)*

29

DESIGNED TO FOLLOW

"I will instruct you and show you the way to go; with my eye on you, I will give counsel." Psalm 32:8

Allison wanted to attend ballet camp and softball camp, but they were happening the same week. She handed the registration sheet to her mom. "What am I going to do? I want to go to both!" she cried.

Mom studied the list of camp options on the registration sheet. Then she looked at Allison. "Let's pray about it together. God might direct you to one or the other, or He might help you know that either one is okay. You can make your choice and then give it your best effort."

Allison and her mom prayed together. Later that night, Allison brought the registration sheet to her mom. Allison had a big smile on her face when she said, "I just need your signature. I know what I want to choose."

TODAY'S SPARK

Choose one of the following creative sparks to do today.

1. Design a maze for friends or family to crawl through. Remember in the maze of life to trust God to lead you where you need to go.

2. Write about a time you had to make a decision between two good things. What did you decide? How did you know what to do?

PRAY

Thank You, God, that You are helping me learn
to trust You in small decisions so I'll know how to trust
You in bigger decisions later. *(Ask God to give you
peace about a decision you might be making now.)*

30

GOD'S DESIGN INCLUDES STOPS AND STARTS

There is an occasion for everything, and a time for every activity under heaven: a time to give birth and a time to die; a time to plant and a time to uproot. *Ecclesiastes 3:1–2*

God has always been here. He has no beginning, and He has no end. He will always exist, and there is nothing outside of His great big plan.

Almost everything else we know has a beginning and an end. We plant seeds and watch them turn into plants. (Then the seed is gone!) We eat the food from the plants and watch the plants die. (Then the plants are gone!) We plant new seeds that the food produced and watch the process start over.

Begin. End. Begin again. God's creation helps us see small examples of His great big plan for His world.

God's plan is for you to be right where you are now. You might not be happy with some of the things around you, but perhaps those things are coming to an end soon, and perhaps that ending will lead to a new beginning! Only God knows everything that will happen, but through it all, you can trust that He is with you.

TODAY'S SPARK

Choose one of the following creative sparks to do today.

1. Draw a picture of your favorite season. Do some research on that time of year. What plants grow then, or what animals do you see the most?

2. Research how to grow a potato or an avocado in a jar, and give it a try. How long before roots begin to form? How long before leaves appear? Take pictures of your plant's growth to document it.

PRAY

God, it's hard to understand how You have always been and always will be since so much is changing in my life. You are eternal, and I worship You. *(Worship God for always being with you, no matter what is going on.)*

GOD PLANS OUR PATH

A person's heart plans his way, but the Lord determines his steps. *Proverbs 16:9*

Nick slumped back in the recliner and stared at the cast on his leg. Summer had just started. Nick had made the summer swim team and had big plans to hang out with his friends. He had hoped to swim for fun and swim for practice. He knew he was stronger this year and couldn't wait for the first competition.

Now this. And it all happened because he had tripped over a rake he'd left out in the backyard. That was the worst part. It was his own fault.

Nick looked up as his nana brought him a glass of lemonade and some cookies. "I know you are more disappointed than I can begin to imagine," Nana said with a soft smile. "But sometimes life's biggest disappointments can be God's way of helping us be where He wants us to be. You may discover that this is a special summer after all."

TODAY'S SPARK

Choose one of the following creative sparks to do today.

1. What might be something good that could come out of Nick's upset plans? Write the next "chapter" of Nick's summer story.

2. Do you know a friend who is having a hard time? Brainstorm some ways to spend time with them, such as playing a game, building a fort, or watching a movie together.

PRAY

God, I can get upset when my plans get messed up.
Help me trust Your plans and be willing to follow You to
places I didn't expect. *(If your life is not going how you
want, ask God to show you how you can still live for Him.)*

32

GOD CALMS OUR FEARS

Do not fear, for I am with you; do not be afraid, for I am your God. I will strengthen you; I will help you; I will hold on to you with my righteous right hand. *Isaiah 41:10*

The children's choir was performing at church on Sunday, and Sadie had a solo. She had practiced and memorized the words, and she was excited to get to sing by herself. But, as Sunday drew closer, she began to feel afraid.

On Sunday morning, she told Mrs. Parker, the choir director, that she was so nervous her knees were shaking! Mrs. Parker sat down in the chair next to Sadie and gave her a quick hug.

"I'm always nervous," Mrs. Parker confessed. Sadie was shocked. "But I've learned two important things," Mrs. Parker continued. "First, feeling nervous just means you want to do a good job, and that's a good thing. Second, I remember Isaiah 41:10, where God says, 'I am your God. I will strengthen you and help you. I will hold on to you.' We can trust God when we are nervous or afraid. He has promised to be our strength."

Sadie smiled and said a quick prayer before taking her spot backstage.

TODAY'S SPARK

Choose one of the following creative sparks to do today.

1. Praying and trusting God are the most important things you can do when you are nervous or afraid. Brainstorm a list of other things that also help, such as taking slow, deep breaths or singing softly to yourself. Write the list down, so you don't forget.

2. Create a rhythm to clap or tap as you say today's verse out loud. Practice the rhythm until you can say the verse by heart.

PRAY

God, You know I am still nervous and afraid even when I am praying. Thank You that when I focus on Your power and strength to help, I begin to feel calmer. *(Tell God a specific thing you are nervous about and ask for His strength in it.)*

33

GOD'S DESIGN WILL BE COMPLETED

"I declare the end from the beginning, and from long ago what is not yet done, saying: my plan will take place, and I will do all my will." *Isaiah 46:10*

Isaiah was one of God's prophets who told the people many of God's messages.

When we read the book of Isaiah, we discover several of God's promises to send a Savior. We also see specific things God said would happen to the Savior. Jesus is the Savior God promised. He fulfilled all the prophecies that were told about Him (Matthew 5:17–18). God was able to give Isaiah those messages because the plan from the very beginning was to send Jesus into the world (2 Timothy 1:9).

Some of Isaiah's prophecies are even about our future. For example, Isaiah wrote that God declared the end from the beginning. In other words, God planned when the world would begin, and He knows how it will end. God promises that His plans will take place. We can trust that this is true because it's always been true before.

Jesus' life proves that!

TODAY'S SPARK

Choose one of the following creative sparks to do today.

1. Cut out a circle about the size of a plate. Begin at the edge and cut a spiral all the way to the center. Write today's verse (Isaiah 46:10) along the spiral. Hang the spinner where a breeze will gently turn it.

2. Create a file of God's promises. Every time you read one in the Bible, write it down on an index card or piece of paper, and file it away. Return to the promises at random times to be encouraged.

PRAY

God, I can feel secure that You are in control of the plans You have for me and for the world. *(Talk to God about anything that is making you feel unsure or insecure right now. Ask Him for assurance that He cares.)*

34

GOD'S DESIGN GIVES HOPE

"I know the plans I have for you"—this is the Lord's declaration—"plans for your well-being, not for disaster, to give you a future and a hope." *Jeremiah 29:11*

The Old Testament includes many descriptions of times the nation of Israel began to follow false gods. When they did, God withdrew His protection, and the people ended up in difficult circumstances. At one point, Babylon attacked Israel and took many of the people into captivity.

After that, God spoke through the prophet Jeremiah with a message of hope for those in captivity. He told them to make lives for themselves in Babylon and to pray that God would bless Babylon—not because Babylon was a good place but because if Babylon did well, so would the Israelites who lived there. God also said that in seventy years, they would return to Jerusalem. Then God made the promise we read in Jeremiah 29:11.

God was giving the people the hope of His promise. As followers of Jesus, we can also be confident that God's plans are always for our good. This gives us hope.

TODAY'S SPARK

Choose one of the following creative sparks to do today.

1. Fold a few sheets of paper together and decorate the cover with the words "My Hope Journal." Keep a record of times when things seem difficult. In the future, look back and add how God helped during those times.

2. Print Jeremiah 29:11, then use art supplies to embellish the words. Add a frame and hang it somewhere to remind you of God's promises.

PRAY

God, You took care of the Israelite nation and kept Your promises to them. *(Thank God for the promises He has kept throughout the generations and for those He will continue to keep.)*

35

GOD'S DESIGN FOR THOSE WHO LOVE HIM

As it is written, What no eye has seen, no ear has heard, and no human heart has conceived—God has prepared these things for those who love him. 1 Corinthians 2:9

Paul is sometimes called "the apostle Paul" because Jesus called him to tell people everywhere the good news about Jesus. Paul traveled to many places and helped start churches. He often wrote letters back to those churches to help them continue to learn about Jesus. Many of those letters are now part of our New Testament. First and Second Corinthians were letters written to the church in Corinth.

The people in Paul's time (and in our time too) sometimes had a hard time understanding why Jesus had to die for our sins. Paul explained that no human could have created a plan to restore our relationship with God. Only God could have created the plan to provide His Son, Jesus, to be our Savior. God did it because He loves us. When we realize what a wonderful plan this was, we love God in return.

TODAY'S SPARK

Choose one of the following creative sparks to do today.

1. Make a "God Loves Me" jar. Cut out heart-shaped pieces of paper or buy a heart-shaped notepad. Write one way you know God loves you, and add it to your jar. Continue to add notes to your jar until it's full.

2. Paul wrote letters that helped people remember God loves them. Who can you write letters to who might need encouragement? Let them know that God loves them and so do you!

PRAY

God, thank You for coming up with the plan to save us through Jesus! No human could have thought of this plan, and I praise You for it. *(Ask God to help you be aware of all the ways He shows His love for you.)*

36

GOD'S DESIGN FOR US AS CHRISTIANS

I see a different law in the parts of my body, waging war against the law of my mind and taking me prisoner to the law of sin in the parts of my body. What a wretched man I am! Who will rescue me from this body of death? Thanks be to God through Jesus Christ our Lord! *Romans 7:23–25*

Jacob tossed his baseball equipment in the car and climbed into the backseat. "What's wrong?" Aunt Marsha asked. She could tell Jacob was upset. Not only was he dirty and sweaty, but he had a huge frown on his face.

"I lost my temper during practice . . . again!" Jacob muttered between clenched teeth. "Coach said I've been doing better, but I still need to work on it. I know I'm a Christian. I know my sins are forgiven. So why do I still get mad? I just keep messing up!"

"God doesn't expect us to be perfect on our own," Aunt Marsha explained. "In fact, He knows we can't. But the Holy Spirit helps you see when you're wrong and invites you to change because He loves you. Hang in there, Jacob. God is always ready to forgive, and He's still working on you."

TODAY'S SPARK

Choose one of the following creative sparks to do today.

1. Rocks can remind us that God has been around for a long time. He's seen a lot of Christians make mistakes. Paint a few rocks with designs to remind you that God loves you—even though you're not perfect. He is still working on you.

2. Doodle a design in the space below. If you mess up, keep going with the design. Think about how nothing, not even our mess-ups and sins, is beyond God's redemption.

PRAY

God, You know my struggles and are there to help me grow. Thank You for sending Jesus so that my sins are forgiven forever! *(Ask God to show you areas of sin you might not be aware of.)*

37
GOD'S WORKMANSHIP

We are his workmanship, created in Christ Jesus for good works, which God prepared ahead of time for us to do. *Ephesians 2:10*

Carly looked up from her study sheet. "Mom," she began, "this week's memory verse is Ephesians 2:10. What does *workmanship* mean?"

"I like that you are thinking about what you are memorizing and not just checking off an assignment!" Mom replied encouragingly. "*Workmanship* means the quality or the result of someone's work or effort. Do you remember how amazing your birthday cake from Miss Kay's bakery looked?"

Carly replied, "It was awesome!"

"Well, the cake didn't decorate itself—it was the result of the quality of work Miss Kay puts into making her cakes. When the Bible says we are God's workmanship, it means He created us and planned good things for us, things that reflect His beautiful love for us."

Carly nodded thoughtfully, "So God created us and is still working to make us something beautiful—makes sense! That reminds me, is there any cake left?"

TODAY'S SPARK

Choose one of the following creative sparks to do today.

1. Sing Ephesians 2:10 to a familiar tune like "Mary Had a Little Lamb." You may also have learned a song to memorize it at Vacation Bible School.

2. Bake and decorate cupcakes. Then write Ephesians 2:10 on paper plates. Place a cupcake on each place, and set them out for your family to enjoy after dinner.

PRAY

God, You made me and are shaping me into the person You want me to be. *(Do you feel special knowing you are God's workmanship? Ask God to help you understand how much you mean to God.)*

38

GOD'S GOOD WORK IN YOU

I am sure of this, that he who started a good work in you will carry it on to completion until the day of Christ Jesus. *Philippians 1:6*

Zach climbed into the truck with Grandpa. The whole family had been at high cousin Adam's medical school graduation. He was going to be a doctor. "I'll bet Adam is super excited to be finished!" Zach exclaimed. "Now he can just be a doctor for the rest of his life."

Grandpa chuckled and replied, "Oh, Adam is just getting started."

"Just getting started?" Zach was confused. "I thought graduation meant you were finished."

"Well, graduation means you have finished the school part. But there are several more steps to complete before Adam can be a doctor. And even after he starts his own practice, he'll keep studying and learning because new discoveries are always happening in the world of medicine."

Zach sat back surprised and thought, *I guess everyone is a work in progress no matter what they've done.*

TODAY'S SPARK

Choose one of the following creative sparks to do today.

1. Pick an activity that takes a while: Make a dessert. Color a complicated coloring page. Edit a video of your family. Or try something else time-consuming. Make sure you complete the project. Remember that God will complete the work He's started in you.

2. Create a workmanship journal: Write down any new things you tried this month (like playing an instrument, baking cookies, or planting flowers). Add a sentence or two about whether you liked it, what you learned, and if you want to keep trying it.

PRAY

God, help me remember that You will complete
the good work You started in me. *(Ask God to help you
recognize the things that fit His design for you.)*

39

GOD'S GOOD PURPOSE FOR YOU

It is God who is working in you both to will and to work according to his good purpose. *Philippians 2:13*

Bethany's dad was a pastor. Some days he let Bethany go with him to visit several of the elderly people from their church at a nursing home. Sometimes they would take cookies Bethany and her mom made, and other times they would take magazines to look through together.

"I'm glad you like to come with me," Dad said one day as they drove to the next visit. "The older people look forward to seeing you."

"I like being with you, Dad," Bethany replied. "And I have fun talking to the people we visit—especially Mr. Dave and Ms. Rosie. They have interesting stories, and it makes me happy when they seem happy."

Dad smiled. "This is good work you are doing. And I wouldn't be surprised if God shows you someday how it prepared you for another good purpose He has in store for you."

TODAY'S SPARK

Choose one of the following creative sparks to do today.

1. Draw a picture of your favorite thing to do. It can be something no one else in your family enjoys. How could God use that for His good purpose?

2. Play with some clay or play dough. As you shape things—mashing the dough back together and shaping something else—think about how God is shaping you for the things He has planned for you. Praise Him for having good purposes for you.

PRAY

God, Your purposes and plans are good. And they include me! *(Ask God to show you how to use the things you enjoy to serve Him and His purposes.)*

40

GOD'S PLAN HAS A PROMISE

You need endurance, so that after you have done God's will, you may receive what was promised. *Hebrews 10:36*

God created an amazing world for us to enjoy with Him. Even though sin broke our relationship with God, we have a way back to Him through Jesus. Humans did not come up with this plan—God did. He is the great designer of our salvation.

And God is eternal: not only is He God of the past and God of the present, but He is also God of the future! Those who believe in Jesus will spend eternity with Him. God promises that this will happen, so we can trust Him. We don't know exactly what the future will be like. But when we look at what God has already created and how much He has done for us, we know it will be awesome!

Until that day, we can remember God is with us and guides us as we follow His plan for our lives. We can trust that what God says—past, present, and future—will come to pass.

TODAY'S SPARK

Choose one of the following creative sparks to do today.

1. You'll probably need your parents' help with this one. Purchase a plain white pair of shoelaces. Decorate them with words or Scriptures that remind you to follow God and trust His promises. Wear the shoelaces or tie them to your backpack as reminders of God's good promises.

2. Sometimes just thinking is being creative. Take a walk outside or look out a window, and think about what you see that reminds you of God. Talk to God about what you see, what you know about Him, and what you are thankful for.

PRAY

Thank You, God, that You aren't finished and that You have plans. *(Thank God for the promises He has already kept and for those He will continue to keep.)*

41

KING OF GLORY

Who is this King of glory? The LORD, strong and mighty, the LORD, mighty in battle. *Psalm 24:8*

King David was one of the most important kings in the Old Testament. King David made lots of mistakes and committed some serious sins, but he was humble before God and admitted when he had done wrong. The Bible says he was a "man after [God's] own heart" (Acts 13:22). Scripture describes David that way because of his strong desire to follow God.

King David also loved music. He wrote many of the *Psalms*, which is a word that means songs. He was a mighty warrior, and his troops were loyal to him. David could have praised himself and written songs about how great he was. Instead, he wrote psalms that focused on the Lord as the ruler of all things.

David knew God was much greater than he was. David was also honest with God. David wrote songs about feeling sad, afraid, angry, mistreated, and lonely. In those moments, David focused his attention on the Lord, the true King of glory.

TODAY'S SPARK

Choose one of the following creative sparks to do today.

1. David was a king who honored the King of all kings—God. Kings often wear a crown. Use aluminum foil to form a crown. You can wear it or put it in your room as a reminder to honor the Lord, the King of glory.

2. David wrote poems telling God how he felt. Write a poem to God telling Him how you are feeling now. End your poem with praise to God like David often did.

PRAY

God, help me remember to honor You. You are mightier than any king who has ever lived, and You deserve all the glory. *(Talk to God about His might and power. If you wrote a poem, read it aloud as a prayer to God.)*

42
PROMISED KING

> A child will be born for us, a son will be given to us, and the government will be on his shoulders. He will be named Wonderful Counselor, Mighty God, Eternal Father, Prince of Peace. *Isaiah 9:6*

Jesus is the *Messiah*, or God's promised King and Deliverer. He is the King God told the prophets He would send. Isaiah is one of the prophets who wrote about the Messiah. When you read Isaiah 9:6, what descriptions help you know something about the Savior God promised?

When the Jewish people read or heard Isaiah's prophecies, they assumed the Messiah would be an earthly ruler. But Jesus didn't come to rule as a king, governor, or president on earth. Jesus came to be the Savior who would restore the broken relationship between God and people.

Jesus' kingdom is a spiritual kingdom. It is both a present kingdom (here, on earth) and an eternal kingdom (forever, in heaven). That's something no earthly king could ever have. But Jesus can, and He does!

TODAY'S SPARK

Choose one of the following creative sparks to do today.

1. Cut a piece of cardboard or poster board about four inches tall and twelve inches wide. Print your name in the middle and add words around your name that describe you. On the other side, print *JESUS*. Add words around His name to describe Him.

2. Glue craft sticks together in the shape of a snowflake. Write several names of Jesus on the sticks. You could use glitter glue or glitter pens. Add a yarn loop for a hanger and use it as a Christmas ornament.

PRAY

Thank You, Jesus, for fulfilling the promise to be our Savior and for ruling over everything, both now and forever.
(Tell Jesus your favorite description of Him and why.)

43

LOVING KING

The LORD is our Judge, the LORD is our Lawgiver, the LORD is our King. He will save us. *Isaiah 33:22*

Brandon and his dad were driving home from church. "Dad," Brandon said, "I'm confused. While I was waiting for you to finish talking to Mr. Harris, I heard another group of people saying how terrible our government is. But the other day, I heard another group of grown-ups talking about what a great job our government is doing. Which is it? They were talking about the same political leaders. I don't get it."

Brandon's dad gave a chuckle and said, "You're going to discover that the more people you meet, the more opinions you'll hear. And most people will be absolutely sure they are right. The truth is, no government is perfect. The Bible tells us to pray for whoever is in power. Thankfully, we know our true ruler is King Jesus. He has proven His love for us, and we can trust His plans for us too."

TODAY'S SPARK

Choose one of the following creative sparks to do today.

1. Draw a self-portrait, which means a picture of yourself. It doesn't have to be perfect—it can even be a cartoon of yourself! Add a crown and think of five rules you would make if you were a king or queen.

2. With an adult's help, build a scepter out of wood, cardboard, or another tough material. Every time you see the scepter, pray for people in power in our country and around the world.

PRAY

God, sometimes the things grown-ups say make me feel worried. Thank You that You are in charge of everything, even the government. *(Pray for any government leaders you know about. Ask God to direct their decisions.)*

44

ETERNAL KING

"You are my witnesses"—this is the LORD's declaration—"and my servant whom I have chosen, so that you may know and believe me and understand that I am he. No god was formed before me, and there will be none after me." *Isaiah 43:10*

Mrs. Jackson watched Maddie and her sister after school. Maddie enjoyed reading her devotional book while Mrs. Jackson sewed. She paused at a word that was new for her and began to sound it out. *E-ter-nal*. "Mrs. Jackson, what does *e-ter-nal* mean?"

Mrs. Jackson thought a minute then asked, "What is the oldest thing you can think of?"

"Grandpa?" Maddie offered.

Mrs. Jackson chuckled. "Older than Grandpa."

Maddie named things like the pioneers, people in Jesus' time, and finally, the beginning of the world. Mrs. Jackson smiled and answered, "Older than that." Maddie looked confused.

Mrs. Jackson explained. "God is *eternal*. That means He was here before anything else was, and He will always be here. It's hard for us to truly understand because most things have beginnings and endings. But God has always been and will always be. He is eternal."

TODAY'S SPARK

Choose one of the following creative sparks to do today.

1. Draw a picture of the oldest thing you can think of. Remember that God created it, and He was around long before it was.

2. Write a definition for *eternal* that someone younger than you could understand. Write a short fiction story about what it would be like to find something eternal.

PRAY

God, it's hard to understand how You have always existed and You will never end. I praise You for being eternal. *(Thank God that people who trust in Jesus as Savior will have eternal life with Him forever.)*

45

COMING KING

Bethlehem Ephrathah, you are small among the clans of
Judah; one will come from you to be ruler over Israel for me.
His origin is from antiquity, from ancient times. *Micah 5:2*

Jesse listened as his dad read the Scripture from their family
Advent devotional. He noticed something he had not thought
about before and asked his dad, "Micah said Bethlehem was
where Jesus would be born hundreds of years before He came.
But why does it matter what town He was born in?"

"That is a great question, Jesse," his dad said. "God put
many prophecies in the Old Testament so when Jesus came,
it would be obvious He was the One God had promised. Also,
Bethlehem was a small town. God often picks the smallest or
least-likely-to-be-chosen places and people to be part of His
plans. This proves God is in control, not people."

Jesse pondered what his dad said. "So God arranged that
Jesus would be born in Bethlehem, even though His family didn't live there. They were from Nazareth but had to go
because of the tax registration. Wow, it's crazy how God works
out the details so that we can see He's in control, not us!"

TODAY'S SPARK

Choose one of the following creative sparks to do today.

1. Draw a simple shape on a piece of paper. Make one for each person who wants to play along. Tell your friends they have three minutes to turn your shape into a drawing. Call time after three minutes and then look at the unexpected results.

2. Bethlehem existed in Micah's time, Jesus' time, and still does today. Look up facts about Bethlehem. How many people lived there when Jesus was born? How many live there now? What does the area around Bethlehem look like?

PRAY

Thank You, God, that You give us so many ways to know You have a plan and You are in control. *(Thank God for Jesus, who came to be the Savior and is coming again someday.)*

46

HUMBLE KING

Look, your King is coming to you; he is righteous and victorious, humble and riding on a donkey, on a colt, the foal of a donkey. *Zechariah 9:9*

Andrea listened as Mr. Jack read the verses for that day's Bible study. Andrea wasn't familiar with Zechariah, but she knew it was a book in the Old Testament. When Mr. Jack read Zechariah 9:9, Andrea raised her hand. "I think this story is about Jesus, but I thought it was in the *New* Testament."

"You're right, Andrea," Mr. Jack encouraged. "Many things Jesus did that are recorded in the New Testament were prophesied, or foretold, in the Old Testament. Remember this verse when we study the story in Matthew in a few weeks."

"But the verse says that the King—that's Jesus—will be righteous, victorious, and humble. The word *humble* sounds kinda weak."

"A lot of people think that," explained Mr. Jack. "But let's think of Jesus' humility as power under control. He did not parade about like a typical king because He came to be our Savior and die on the cross for sins."

TODAY'S SPARK

Choose one of the following creative sparks to do today.

1. Old Testament prophets didn't have computers like we do today. They wrote with quills or reeds. So try writing like a prophet. Snip the end of a drinking straw at an angle. Then make a tiny snip at the point. Dip the point in paint and write on a piece of paper.

2. Be a Bible detective. Watch for Old Testament Scriptures that show up in the New Testament, such as prophecies that are fulfilled, or when New Testament authors quote the Old Testament. Keep a list in your journal. (Hint: Today's verse will connect with a devotion you will read soon.)

PRAY

God, Your Word is amazing. Thank You for guiding writers to write down exactly what we need to learn, and thank You for keeping Your promises. *(Ask God to help you learn more as you study your Bible.)*

47

FUTURE KING

On that day the LORD will become King over the whole earth—
the LORD alone, and his name alone. *Zechariah 14:9*

Some people think Revelation is the only book in the Bible that talks about Jesus' return. But did you know there are several prophecies in the Old Testament that tell about things that still haven't happened yet? You read one of those prophecies today.

Zechariah is the next to the last book in the Old Testament. In today's verse, Zechariah told the people of God's plan to return and reign over the whole earth. He also wrote that "the LORD alone" and "his name alone" would be exalted over all the earth.

There is only one true God. People who lived long before Zechariah and people who live long after him have been warned not to worship any other god or treat anything as more important than the Lord. When we worship God and follow Him, we can trust His promise to be our King forever.

TODAY'S SPARK

Choose one of the following creative sparks to do today.

1. How many Bible book names do you know? Write each book on craft sticks, sticky notes, or index cards. Then see how fast you can sort the Old Testament and New Testament book names. Use the table of contents in the front of your Bible to help.

2. Zechariah gave an encouraging message to some discouraged Israelites. Write a note to someone who needs encouragement. You can buy a card or make one yourself.

PRAY

God, the Bible proves You keep Your promises. Thank You that we can trust You to keep the great promises still to come. *(Ask Jesus to help you know how to follow Him now as you look forward to His return.)*

48

BIRTH OF THE KING

After Jesus was born in Bethlehem of Judea in the days of King Herod, wise men from the east arrived in Jerusalem, saying, "Where is he who has been born king of the Jews? For we saw his star at its rising and have come to worship him." *Matthew 2:1–2*

Antonio enjoyed reading aloud to his great-grandma since she could no longer see to read for herself. When he read about the wise men, Antonio had some questions. "Great-Grandma, who were the wise men? Were they super smart? How did they know about Jesus? Where did they come from?"

"I'm so glad you are thinking about what you are reading!" said Great-Grandma. "The wise men were also called *magi*. They lived far away from Jerusalem in a different country. They were called wise because they studied many things, including religions, and asked questions like you do."

Great-Grandma continued, "Because of their studies, the wise men knew a king had been born, and they wanted to find Him. God had revealed a special star to guide them on their journey to Jesus. It led them all the way to the house where Jesus was as a child. And even though they were important men, the magi bowed and worshiped Jesus because they knew He was much more important."

TODAY'S SPARK

Choose one of the following creative sparks to do today.

1. Use a sheet of black construction paper and white chalk or white crayon to draw a night sky. Add what you think the special star the wise men followed might have looked like. Write the words of Matthew 2:2 on your picture.

2. Pretend you were one of the wise men who went to find Jesus. Write about your experience traveling toward Him and then finally seeing Him.

PRAY

Thank You, God, for arranging amazing things— like the special star—so people can know about You. Help me to have a heart of worship! (*Pray for people you know who need to know about King Jesus.*)

49

THE KING AND HIS KINGDOM

"You should pray like this: Our Father in heaven, your name be honored as holy. Your kingdom come. Your will be done on earth as it is in heaven." *Matthew 6:9–10*

Jesus taught His disciples many things while He was with them. They often saw Jesus slip away to be alone and pray to their heavenly Father. The disciples asked Jesus to teach them to pray. Matthew 6:9–13 records what some people call "the Lord's Prayer," and others call "the Model Prayer." Jesus gave us an example of how to talk to God.

Jesus' model begins with "Our Father in heaven, your name be honored as holy." This reminds us of who God is and shows Him honor. Then Jesus taught the disciples to ask that God's kingdom would come. While Jesus was on earth, He demonstrated what God's kingdom is like—it is full of grace, truth, compassion, and more. Someday, when God creates a new heaven and a new earth, His kingdom will be complete, and, as believers, we will be a part of that kingdom.

TODAY'S SPARK

Choose one of the following creative sparks to do today.

1. Type the words of the Lord's Prayer. Choose a font you like and make it large enough to fill most of the page. Print out the page, then decorate around the words with different media (colored pencils, paints, buttons, tissue paper, and so on).

2. Jesus found quiet places to pray. To help you remember to have quiet times with God, make a quiet-time box. Place things in your box such as your Bible, a devotional book, a prayer journal, and a pen. Decorate the box. Leave it in your room or take it with you when you travel.

PRAY

Jesus, thank You for setting the example for us about how to pray. Help me prioritize praying to You more. *(Talk to Jesus about how His example helps you know prayer is important.)*

50

UNEXPECTED KING

Tell Daughter Zion, "See, your King is coming to you, gentle, and mounted on a donkey, and on a colt, the foal of a donkey." *Matthew 21:5*

Do you remember a recent devotion that focused on the prophecy from Zechariah 9:9 in the Old Testament? Isn't it amazing to read this passage in Matthew 21 from the New Testament and see it happening?

The two books of the Bible may be just a few pages apart, but hundreds of years passed between the prophecy in Zechariah and the event in Matthew. And it happened exactly as God said it would! Jesus rode into Jerusalem on the colt of a donkey. Most kings in that time would have paraded into town on the grandest stallion, adorned with kingly garments and saddle. But Jesus rode on a lowly animal. He was dressed no different than any other day, and the donkey only had some cloaks the disciples had tossed over its back as a makeshift saddle.

The people expected the Messiah to be a conquering hero, so Jesus' arrival was not what they expected. Jesus was completely obedient to God's plan—the one the prophets spoke of in the Old Testament—down to the very last detail.

TODAY'S SPARK

Choose one of the following creative sparks to do today.

1. Jesus' arrival in Jerusalem was unexpected for the people. Have you ever seen anything unexpected? Write about the experience in your journal. Make sure to include all the emotions and details.

2. Explore related Bible passages. Copy Zechariah 9:9 on the left-hand side of a page and Matthew 21:5 on the right. Draw lines connecting exact words that match from one verse to the other. Draw squiggly lines connecting words that mean almost the same thing in each verse.

PRAY

Jesus, thank You for helping us know You are truly the Messiah. You followed God's plan to the very last detail. *(Talk to Jesus about other things you've learned that show He is the One God promised.)*

51

BLESSED KING

The crowds who went ahead of him and those who followed shouted: "Hosanna to the Son of David! Blessed is he who comes in the name of the Lord! Hosanna in the highest heaven!" *Matthew 21:9*

In the previous devotion, you read about how Jesus entered Jerusalem on a donkey. If you read further, you'll notice what the crowds of people were doing as Jesus entered the city. Once again, there is a connection between the Old Testament and the New Testament. The people shouted words we can find in Psalm 118:25–26. The word *hosanna* means "save us"! After that, the people declared, "Blessed is he who comes in the name of the Lord!"

This entry into Jerusalem happened about a week before Jesus was crucified. Jesus knew what was about to happen, but His followers did not. On that day, the crowds were cheering and greeting Jesus with praises. But before the week was over, crowds would be shouting for His death.

Jesus continued to be obedient to God's design no matter what the crowds wanted. The people were right to call Jesus blessed, and we are blessed because of Jesus.

TODAY'S SPARK

Choose one of the following creative sparks to do today.

1. Have you ever made a fingerprint picture? Use stamp pads or pour small amounts of paint on a disposable plate. Dip your fingertip onto the pad or paint, and then illustrate a scene from Matthew 21:8–9 with it.

2. Print *Hosanna* on a sheet of paper using bubble letters. Across the bottom, write down what you want Jesus to save you from.

PRAY

Jesus, You knew what would happen to You, and You still followed God's plan. Thank You for not being swayed by the crowds and for dying on the cross for me. *(Read Psalm 118:25–26 as a prayer. Tell Jesus the reasons He is blessed.)*

52

KING OF TRUTH

"You have said it," Jesus told him. "But I tell you, in the future
you will see the Son of Man seated at the right hand of Power
and coming on the clouds of heaven." *Matthew 26:64*

Michelle found her dad pulling weeds outside in the yard.
"Dad, can I ask you a question?"

"Sure, sweetie, what's up?" Dad replied as he worked.

"My Bible reading today is about the night Jesus was
arrested when He was brought before the *Sanhedrin*, or the
religious leaders at the time. Why didn't Jesus tell them who
He was? It says He stayed silent."

Dad looked up. "Jesus knew He had come to be our Savior,
and the things that were happening needed to take place.
Isaiah even prophesied hundreds of years earlier that the
Messiah would keep silent."

He went on, "So when the high priest asked if Jesus was the
Messiah, the Son of God, Jesus only said, 'You have said it,' to
the high priest. He would not speak in His defense, but He still
spoke truthfully. The best part of this story is that Jesus said
one day we would see Him coming on the clouds of heaven.
That's something you and I can look forward to!"

TODAY'S SPARK

Choose one of the following creative sparks to do today.

1. Jesus the King will return on the clouds one day. Use a blue sheet of construction paper. Tear cotton balls into wisps and glue them to the paper to spell *KING*, or if you have room, *KING JESUS*.

2. Compare Daniel 7:13 and Matthew 26:64. If you were a news reporter, how would you share this information? Ask a grown-up to record your news report on a smartphone or other device.

PRAY

Jesus, I know the night of trials was so difficult for You.
Thank You for being faithful to fulfill God's plan as our
Savior. *(Jesus was willing to endure so much because
He loves you. Tell Jesus what that means to you.)*

53

KINGDOM OF GOD

"My kingdom is not of this world," said Jesus. "If my kingdom were of this world, my servants would fight, so that I wouldn't be handed over to the Jews. But as it is, my kingdom is not from here." *John 18:36*

After Michelle and her dad talked about Jesus' trial before the Sanhedrin, they began to discuss Jesus' time with the Roman governor, Pilate. "Why did the religious leaders take Jesus to the Roman governor?" Michelle asked.

"The Romans who ruled Judea would not allow the Jews to execute people—only Rome could do that," Dad explained. "But the religious leaders were so angry, they wanted Jesus killed. It sounds terrible and it was, but Jesus knew His purpose was to die for our sins. Pilate even asked Jesus why His own people had arrested Him."

Michelle's dad then showed her John 18:36 in the Bible. "This is what Jesus replied. People kept imagining an earthly kingdom with an earthly ruler. But Jesus knew His kingdom was so much bigger—it is not limited to this world! If Jesus was only a King over this earthly kingdom, He might have stopped everything that was happening. But Jesus knew He had a purpose for eternity and a heavenly kingdom."

TODAY'S SPARK

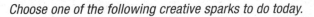

Choose one of the following creative sparks to do today.

1. Design a shield with imagery that represents a heavenly kingdom. Cut the shape from cardboard. Draw designs with bottled glue, and allow them to dry. The glue should stay raised. Cover the shield with aluminum foil and rub gently until the design shows.

2. Do a follow-up investigative reporter interview. Compare John 18:36 with what happened back in John 6:15. What conclusions can you draw for your report?

PRAY

Jesus, thank You for teaching us about Your kingdom. I'm glad You were not an earthly ruler, but You are a heavenly one. *(Thank Jesus for the blessing of being part of His kingdom.)*

54

LORD AND KING

"Let all the house of Israel know with certainty that God has made this Jesus, whom you crucified, both Lord and Messiah." *Acts 2:36*

Carlos took his Bible off the shelf in his room and looked up the passage Mr. Patterson had written on a sticky note. In church, Carlos had asked his Bible study leader how he could know for sure Jesus was who Christians said He was. Carlos found Acts 2, began reading at verse 14, and continued reading through Peter's sermon. When Carlos got to verse 36, he was surprised, and he read it again.

Those words "know with certainty" got Carlos's attention. Peter, who had followed Jesus throughout His ministry on earth and who had seen Him after He rose from the dead, knew with certainty who Jesus was. He was the Messiah God had promised and Lord of all. In his preaching, Peter was helping the people know that too.

Carlos kept reading and learned that about three thousand people became believers after hearing Peter's sermon. *Now that's proof worth believing!* Carlos thought to himself.

TODAY'S SPARK

Choose one of the following creative sparks to do today.

1. Do you believe Jesus is who He says He is? Why or why not? If you do, write a song of praise using the words *Lord* and *Messiah*.

2. If you were going to teach someone about Jesus, what would you say? Practice on your stuffed animal or your pet. Then, when you feel more comfortable, try telling what you know to someone who is willing to listen.

PRAY

God, thank You that I can read the Bible and know for certain who Jesus is. *(Talk to God about any other questions you might have.)*

55

RULER OVER ALL

He [God] exercised this power in Christ by raising him from the dead and seating him at his right hand in the heavens—far above every ruler and authority, power and dominion, and every title given, not only in this age but also in the one to come. *Ephesians 1:20–21*

Throughout history, nations and countries have had many types of rulers. They were given various titles like king, emperor, president, or pharaoh. They had power to make decisions that affected every person who lived under their rule. Some were kind and good. They tried to make decisions that helped those they were responsible for. Others were evil and were willing to hurt their own people to get what they wanted.

All those rulers (and those that will become rulers in the future) are simply human beings like you and me. They might have power for a period of time, but they eventually lose power or die. Only One has ever lived who is above every other ruler or authority. That One is Jesus. He rose from the dead to show His power over life and death. He is ruler over all now and forever!

TODAY'S SPARK

Choose one of the following creative sparks to do today.

1. Many artists listen to music to inspire them. Listen to music that praises the mighty power of Jesus. Doodle while you listen. What did you create?

2. With sidewalk chalk, write *POWER* on the driveway or sidewalk outside. Use the letters in *POWER* to create an acrostic of words or phrases that describe Jesus.

PRAY

Jesus, You are ruler over all. There is no one like You, for You are the Son of God. I praise Your name! *(Think about how Jesus, the ruler of everything, knows you and loves you. Tell Jesus how you feel when you think about that.)*

56

ONE AND ONLY KING

Now to the King eternal, immortal, invisible, the only God, be honor and glory forever and ever. Amen. *1 Timothy 1:17*

Emily could hear her grandma singing in the kitchen while she cooked breakfast, but Emily didn't recognize the song. She stepped into the kitchen and listened a bit longer. Finally, she asked, "Grandma, what are you singing? I don't think I've heard it before."

Grandma chuckled. "Oh, it's a song we sang in church when I was growing up. It always made me happy because it reminds us that Jesus is the eternal King." Grandma began to sing, "He is immortal, invisible, God only wise." Grandma finished the song and smiled. "I like to think about how great Jesus is first thing in the morning. When I sing praises to Him, my day starts out right."

Emily smiled back. "I like that! Just listening to you makes me feel happier. It reminds me that God is awesome. Can you teach me that song?"

TODAY'S SPARK

Choose one of the following creative sparks to do today.

1. Create a word search by using a piece of graph paper—or a page with squares—to keep the letters straight. Use some of the words from 1 Timothy 1:17. Include other words that describe Jesus. Add a word box so you can keep track of what words are included. Give it to someone who enjoys word puzzles!

2. Brainstorm a list of things in creation that are invisible but still important. Are any of these things powerful? Why? Are they eternal or immortal?

PRAY

Jesus, we honor You when we sing praises to You, and praising You helps lift my spirits too! *(Spend time praising Jesus in a creative way for being the eternal, immortal, invisible, and the only God. Ask a friend to join you.)*

57

KING OF KINGS

He is the blessed and only Sovereign, the King of kings, and the Lord of lords. *1 Timothy 6:15*

The verse for today is from a letter the apostle Paul wrote to Timothy. Paul had mentored Timothy and helped him grow in his knowledge about Jesus and God's kingdom. Timothy had even traveled on some missionary journeys with Paul and learned a lot from Paul's teaching.

At times, Paul would leave Timothy in charge of a church they had started. Paul often wrote to Timothy to encourage him, reminding him that they were serving the King of kings and Lord of lords, the One who is blessed and sovereign. *Sovereign* means someone who has power or authority over everything.

Serving the Lord and telling people about Jesus can be challenging. Paul understood that. (Read 2 Corinthians 11:23–33 to see some of the trials Paul went through.) But Paul wanted Timothy to be encouraged. No matter what happened to them, they belonged to the King of kings.

TODAY'S SPARK

Choose one of the following creative sparks to do today.

1. Turn a sheet of paper sideways and fan-fold it into three sections. Trace a paper doll outline with the hands connected and cut it out. Decorate the first paper doll in the chain to represent someone who told you about Jesus. Decorate the second paper doll to look like you. Decorate the third paper doll as someone you can tell about Jesus.

2. Paul wrote letters to Timothy to encourage him. Type an email encouraging a believer to keep telling others about Jesus. Ask for permission from your parents before sending the email.

PRAY

God, thank You for people who taught me about You and Your Son, Jesus. Give me the courage to tell others about Him too! *(Pray for each person you can think of who has helped you know more about Jesus.)*

58

PRAISE TO THE KING

Jesus Christ, the faithful witness, the firstborn from the dead and the ruler of the kings of the earth. To him who loves us and has set us free from our sins by his blood, and made us a kingdom, priests to his God and Father—to him be glory and dominion forever and ever. *Revelation 1:5–6*

Revelation is the last book in the Bible. John, one of the original twelve disciples, was very old and had been exiled to, or imprisoned on, an island called Patmos. John could not leave, but he was able to send letters while he was there. So he wrote to churches and told them things God had shown them.

John began this letter by reminding the churches about who Jesus is: Jesus is risen from the dead. He rules over all the earth. He loves us and has provided forgiveness for our sins through His sacrifice. Because of Jesus, those who trust Him as Savior become part of God's kingdom forever. Jesus deserves all praise!

A couple of verses later, John described Jesus as being the Alpha and the Omega, the One who is, who was, and who is to come (verse 8). *Alpha* means "first," and *omega* means "last." John is saying Jesus is not just a man—He is the eternal God.

TODAY'S SPARK

Choose one of the following creative sparks to do today.

1. Imagine you've been exiled on an island. Write a story or draw a picture about what that would be like. What would you do to pass the time? What enemies might you encounter?

2. Write a letter with real paper and pen telling a friend something you've learned recently about Jesus. If you can, mail the letter.

PRAY

Jesus, thank You for the reminders of how awesome You are. I praise You, Almighty King, who has dominion forever and ever! *(Tell Jesus how it makes you feel that He is the Alpha and Omega, the first and the last.)*

59

THE KING WILL REIGN FOREVER

The seventh angel blew his trumpet, and there were loud voices in heaven saying, "The kingdom of the world has become the kingdom of our Lord and of his Christ, and he will reign forever and ever." *Revelation 11:15*

Andrew muttered, "*Why* do I have to go to this old concert?"

Andrew's mom heard his grumbling. "Handel's *Messiah* is a music composition largely based on Bible passages. And the 'Hallelujah Chorus' is pretty famous. Let me show you."

Andrew's mom took him to the piano where she had a copy of the *Messiah*. She opened to the "Hallelujah Chorus" and turned to the book of Revelation in her Bible. "The chorus begins with an exciting round of hallelujah praises, and then these words: *For the Lord God Omnipotent reigneth.* Now look at Revelation 19:6. The composer used these words to praise God."

Andrew's mom pointed out another part of the chorus: *The kingdom of this world is become the kingdom of our Lord and of His Christ, and He will reign forever and ever.*

Andrew got excited. "That's Revelation 11:15. I read it in my devotion today!" Andrew grabbed his jacket. Maybe this concert would be fun after all.

Choose one of the following creative sparks to do today.

1. A famous part of Handel's *Messiah* is known as the "Hallelujah Chorus." Ask someone to play it for you, or find it online on a streaming service. While you listen, keep your eyes on Revelation 11:15, and see if you recognize the words.

2. Revelation 11:15 is an announcement by heavenly voices. Write the verse on construction paper, then roll the paper up like a megaphone. Read the announcement part of the verse while holding the megaphone to your mouth.

PRAY

Jesus, I know You will reign forever. Whenever things get hard in life, help me remember that! *(Praise God for His kingdom and His promises.)*

60

CONQUERING KING

The Lamb will conquer them because he is the Lord of lords and the King of kings. Those with him are called, chosen, and faithful. Revelation 17:14

Do you remember when you read the Old Testament prophecy about Jesus coming into Jerusalem on a donkey (Zechariah 9:9)? Then you read about when it happened in the New Testament (Matthew 21:5)?

The people truly thought Jesus was coming to overthrow Rome and take the earthly throne as king. They didn't understand Jesus came to take on the punishment for sin so we could have a restored relationship with God. Even Jesus' disciples were confused and ran away after He was arrested (Mark 14:50).

But Jesus stuck to God's plan: He took the punishment for sin when He died on the cross, and He defeated death when He rose from the grave three days later.

But God's design will not be complete until Jesus establishes His new heaven and new earth. Then Jesus ("the Lamb" from today's verse) will be the conquering hero, and those who trust Jesus as Savior will be part of His eternal kingdom. Praise be to the Lord!

TODAY'S SPARK

Choose one of the following creative sparks to do today.

1. Place a piece of aluminum foil over something with texture (bubble wrap, net vegetable bags, tree bark, several coins in a flat layer on the table, etc.). Rub gently until you have an embossed image pressed into the foil. Cut a sheep shape from it. Tape it to a sheet of construction paper and write "The Lamb will conquer them." on your artwork.

2. Ask your parents to take you to a petting zoo where you can take photos of donkeys and sheep. Think about how Jesus rode into Jerusalem on a donkey and became "the Lamb," or the sacrifice for our sins.

PRAY

Jesus, Your kingdom is forever! God's design to save the world through You did not fail in the past, and it never will fail. *(Talk to Jesus about how it makes you feel to be part of His forever kingdom.)*

61

WHAT IS A REDEEMER?

Boaz said to the elders and all the people, "You are witnesses today that I am buying from Naomi everything that belonged to Elimelech, Chilion, and Mahlon." *Ruth 4:9*

Ashley looked up from her vocabulary list. "Mom," she asked, "The word *redeem* is on my list this week. The meaning is "to regain possession of something in exchange for payment." Can you explain it to me?"

"Sure," Mom began. "*Regain possession* means this is something the person used to have but doesn't anymore. *Redeem* means a price must be paid to get that thing back. Do you remember the story of Ruth in the Bible?" Ashley nodded. "Naomi could not afford to keep her husband's property, but a family member was allowed to pay for it and redeem it for the family. Boaz redeemed the property, then he married Ruth. Did you know that King David was the great-grandson of Boaz and Ruth?"

Ashley shook her head. "That's cool," she said.

"And Jesus came from the line of David. Jesus is the ultimate Redeemer because He took our punishment and paid the price for sin, which we could never pay. Now we can be a part of God's family!"

TODAY'S SPARK

Choose one of the following creative sparks to do today.

1. New purpose often follows redemption. Find an empty water bottle. What are some things you can do with the water bottle to give it new purpose?

2. God gave Naomi and Ruth family to help them. Think about the people God has placed around you. Draw three circles inside each other (like a target). Write your name in the center. In the next circle list the people who live with you and care for you. In the outer circle, list people who live near you and sometimes care for you. Print the name GOD at the top of the page. Thank Him for the people around you.

PRAY

God, thank You for family. But most of all, thank You for Jesus, who is my Redeemer. *(Pray for family members by name and thank God for them.)*

62

CONFIDENCE IN OUR REDEEMER

I know that my Redeemer lives, and at the end he will stand on the dust. *Job 19:25*

Caleb dribbled the basketball across the driveway. Mr. Gibson was sitting nearby. "Hey there, Caleb," he said. "I'm sure going to miss your basketball skills when you move."

Caleb dropped down next to Mr. Gibson. "I hate moving and starting a new school." He looked at his shoes. "It feels like a lot of bad stuff is happening at the same time."

Mr. Gibson nodded. "Life is like that sometimes. It makes me think of Job in the Bible. So many bad things happened at once. His friends wondered if he had done something wrong, but Job was just going through a time of suffering. Finally Job told his friends, 'I know my Redeemer lives'!"

"Why would he say that?" asked Caleb.

"Job had confidence in God, his Redeemer, and you can too. You've trusted in Jesus as Savior, which is the greatest redemption. But Jesus also can redeem this time for you." He gave Caleb a hug. "Trust God, and He'll see you through."

TODAY'S SPARK

Choose one of the following creative sparks to do today.

1. The book of Job is a type of poem. You can look it up in your Bible. Write a poem of your own about what you know about Jesus, the Redeemer. Your poem can rhyme or not.

2. Sometimes when things are going badly, it's helpful to focus on what we're grateful for. Grab a phone or camera and take pictures of things you love—either indoors or outdoors. Scroll through the pictures and thank God for what's in each image.

PRAY

Dear God, thank You that we can say along with Job,
"I know my Redeemer lives!" *(Talk to God about
things that are troubling you, and then pray for
peace and confidence in your Redeemer.)*

63

HONORING OUR REDEEMER

May the words of my mouth and the meditation of my heart be acceptable to you, Lord, my rock and my Redeemer. *Psalm 19:14*

Coach Hansel pulled Evan aside after the game. "I know you are upset about our team losing today, but that doesn't give you permission to say hateful things to the other team."

"But Coach!" Evan exclaimed. "They were cheating!"

Coach Hansel put his hand on Evan's shoulder. "Regardless of what we think others do, we are responsible for our own actions. Our team has said we want to honor Christ in what we do. I pray the words of Psalm 19:14 every day, and I mean them. I want my words and my thoughts to be acceptable to the Lord, who is my Redeemer."

Evan sighed and finally muttered, "You're right, Coach. I need to trust you to speak up for our team, and I need to ask God to help me watch my mouth." He took a deep breath. "And I guess I need to apologize to their coach."

TODAY'S SPARK

Choose one of the following creative sparks to do today.

1. Sometimes athletes add a Scripture reference on their caps to show what they believe. Use the outline below to design a cap that helps show what you believe.

2. Words can tear people down or build people up. With that in mind, gather a jar full of blocks. Each day you say something to build someone up, take a block from the jar, and include it as part of a growing sculpture. If you catch yourself using your words to tear someone down, remove a block and return it to the jar. Your tower can help you remember to be careful with your words.

PRAY

Dear God, may the words of my mouth and the meditation of my heart be acceptable to You, my Rock and my Redeemer. *(Talk to God about the times it is hard to control your words.)*

64

PRAISE TO THE REDEEMER

My lips will shout for joy when I sing praise to you because you have redeemed me. *Psalm 71:23*

Nolan loved spending time in the summer at his granddad's house. The old house creaked and had odd smells that Nolan found strangely comforting. One day Nolan's granddad was sitting at the kitchen table looking through a box of old items. "What's that?" Nolan asked

"I found this box of my dad's things," Granddad said.

"You mean my *great*-granddad?" Nolan asked.

"That's right. I found some letters he kept and some old photos. But look, here is his Bible. He had a bookmark at Psalm 71, marking verses 17 and 18. Those verses are about telling future generations about God's power. We are here reading his notes, so I guess he is," Granddad chuckled.

Nolan ran his fingers over the edge of the thin paper as Granddad continued, "Verse 23 is one of my favorites because it reminds me that God's love always gives us a reason to celebrate. I can shout for joy and sing praise because my Savior has redeemed me."

TODAY'S SPARK

Choose one of the following creative sparks to do today.

1. Make a Bible bookmark to remember a special verse in your Bible. Cut a strip of construction paper and decorate it with stickers. You can write a favorite verse on the bookmark too. Cover the bookmark with clear packing tape to protect it.

2. What praise songs make you want to clap your hands or dance for joy? Sing aloud to God and show your praise.

PRAY

God, I praise You. No matter what's going on,
Your love always gives me a reason to rejoice!
(Tell God why you want to celebrate Him.)

65

ONE GOD

I am the LORD. Besides me,
there is no Savior. *Isaiah 43:11*

If you read much of the Old Testament, you will notice that God reminds people over and over that He is the one and only God. In fact, the first three commandments are all about worshiping only God. Why do you think God kept reminding people of this?

God created us, and He created the world we enjoy. He loves us and takes care of us. It's hard to imagine why people would want to think something else is a god, but many of the Old Testament writers talked about how people took pieces of wood and carved them into an idol before burning the rest to keep warm (Isaiah 44:12–20).

We may not carve an image out of wood and pray to it today, but we do let things become more important than God. That's basically the same thing! God wants to be our only God. There is no other god but our one true God.

TODAY'S SPARK

Choose one of the following creative sparks to do today.

1. Tape eight craft sticks side by side and flip them over. Write Isaiah 43:11 across the sticks and decorate with markers so that each stick has part of the verse on it. Pull the tape off, and put the sticks in a sandwich bag. Share your puzzle with a friend to rearrange in order.

2. Grab a large, wide rubber band or turn a silicone bracelet inside out so you can write on the inside. With a permanent marker, write Isaiah 43:11 on the inside to serve as a reminder to serve God above all else.

PRAY

God, I am sorry I sometimes forget how important You are. Please help me honor You in all I do. *(Ask God to help you know when you forget to put Him first).*

66

LONG-AWAITED REDEEMER

At that very moment, she came up and began to thank God and to speak about him to all who were looking forward to the redemption of Jerusalem. *Luke 2:38*

Ella marked another day off the calendar before crawling into bed. She only had three more days before her family's camping trip, and she could hardly wait! Just then her mom came in to read the Bible with her. When she sat down on the edge of her bed, Ella exclaimed, "I'm so excited! Don't you think it's hard to wait for something special?"

"I do," agreed Mom. "It's fun to be excited. And I know what we can read about tonight. It's the story of a woman named Anna, who had waited for something very special for a long time. In fact, she had lived and served in the temple for many years. When Mary and Joseph brought baby Jesus to the temple, Anna knew He was the Messiah God had promised would bring redemption. She was *really* excited!"

"I'd like to hear more about Anna," Ella said. "Let's read that story tonight."

TODAY'S SPARK

Choose one of the following creative sparks to do today.

1. Write about a time you looked forward to something and then couldn't believe it when it finally happened.

2. Learn more about Anna's story. Read Luke 2:22–38, then write a script so you can reenact the story with your siblings or friends.

PRAY

God, I can celebrate just like Anna that You sent Jesus. *(Ask God to help you share your excitement with your friends.)*

67

CHILDREN OF GOD

To all who did receive him, he gave them the right to be children of God, to those who believe in his name. *John 1:12*

Owen had recently trusted Jesus as his Savior. He had been attending a new believers' class and was excited about his upcoming baptism day. He opened his *New Christian's Workbook* the church had given him and read the verse for the day.

"Dad," he asked, "What does it mean that when we believe in Jesus' name, we have the right to be children of God? I thought God made everyone."

"God did create the world and everyone in it," Dad replied. "But sin separated us from God. When we trust Jesus as Savior, we are redeemed, or bought back, and we become part of the family of God. Being a child of God also means we are brothers and sisters in Christ."

Owen's face lit up. "So everyone who is a Christian is my brother or sister? Wow, I have a big family!"

TODAY'S SPARK

Choose one of the following creative sparks to do today.

1. Think of people you know who are Christians. Create a "family portrait" by drawing a stick figure for every person you can think of, and write the name by each stick figure. Can you fill a sheet of paper with people you know who are part of the family of God?

2. Make up a song about believing in Jesus. Try to use "child of God" or "family of God" in the lyrics.

PRAY

Thank You, God, for making me part of
Your family when I trusted in Jesus as Savior.
*(Thank God for helping you understand about
becoming a Christian and what that means for your life.)*

68

BECAUSE GOD LOVES US

God loved the world in this way: He gave his one and only Son, so that everyone who believes in him will not perish but have eternal life. *John 3:16*

Have you ever seen people hold up signs at sporting events that say, "John 3:16"?

Why do you think people want others to know about that verse? Some people think it's the simplest way to share the gospel, or the good news, about Jesus. Have you ever tried to summarize the gospel? Here is a simple way:

Creation: God created the world, including people, and it was perfect.

Fall: Sin broke the relationship people had with God.

Redemption: God loved people so much, He could not leave things broken. He sent Jesus into the world to die on the cross, taking the punishment for our sins. Three days later, Jesus rose from the dead!

Restoration: Those who believe in Jesus and receive His gift of forgiveness have the eternal life He provides, now and forever. Because of Jesus, we can always ask for forgiveness and enjoy a restored relationship with our heavenly Father.

TODAY'S SPARK

Choose one of the following creative sparks to do today.

1. Write each word of John 3:16 on separate sticky notes. Scatter the notes around the room. Use a stopwatch app to see how fast you, or your siblings, can put the verse in order.

2. Read the full story of today's Bible verse in John 3:1–21. Make two paper bag puppets, and act out the conversation between Nicodemus and Jesus.

PRAY

God, thank You for giving us the Bible to show us Your love through the gospel. *(Ask God to help you memorize John 3:16 to remember what Jesus did and the forgiveness you find in Him.)*

69

JESUS IS THE REDEEMER

Jesus told him, "I am the way, the truth, and the life. No one comes to the Father except through me." *John 14:6*

Sophia stayed after Bible class to talk to Mrs. Arnold. "I'm sorry I asked so many questions today," Sophia said.

Mrs. Arnold gave Sophia a warm smile and replied, "I love your questions, Sophia. The more you ask, the better you understand. Even one of Jesus' disciples, Thomas, was known for his questions."

"Really?" asked Sophia.

Mrs. Arnold continued. "One time, Jesus told His disciples He was leaving to prepare a place for them, but Thomas was confused. He asked how they would know where to go. Jesus said, 'I am the way, the truth, and the life.' Thomas still didn't understand, but that was okay. Later on he did: Jesus' sacrifice on the cross was the way back to God."

"So you're saying when I ask questions, sometimes I'll get answers right away, and sometimes I won't until later."

"That's right," said Mrs. Arnold. "Ask any question. Jesus understands and welcomes them."

TODAY'S SPARK

Choose one of the following creative sparks to do today.

1. Print today's verse on the front of a folded card. Dip the handle end of a paintbrush in paint and make dot patterns around the verse. On the inside, write a note to a friend about Jesus.

2. Create a maze on paper for someone else to solve. Make sure there is only one way from start to finish. At the bottom of the maze, write today's verse.

PRAY

God, thank You for not minding when I have questions. In fact, You welcome them! *(Talk to God about things you are unsure of and ask Him to help you wait for the answers.)*

70

THE PROOF AROUND US

His invisible attributes, that is, his eternal power and divine nature, have been clearly seen since the creation of the world, being understood through what he has made. As a result, people are without excuse. *Romans 1:20*

Arthur said he's never heard of Jesus!" Aiden exclaimed to his older brother. "I've known about Jesus all my life. How can anyone not know about Jesus?"

"I know it's shocking," Aiden's brother replied. "But if someone has never been to church or had someone around who talks about Jesus, they may not know who He is."

"But I thought the Bible said there is evidence everywhere," Aiden said, still trying to figure things out.

"Evidence of God is everywhere," Aiden's brother agreed. "But those of us who know God's Son, Jesus, are invited to tell others about Him. If Arthur has told you he has never heard of Jesus, it probably means God is giving you the opportunity to share your faith with him, which is exciting!"

TODAY'S SPARK

Choose one of the following creative sparks to do today.

1. Cover a piece of cardstock or heavy paper with oil pastels or crayons, using pressure as you color. Mix a small amount of water with black acrylic paint, and paint over the coloring to hide all the colors. After the paint dries, use a wooden skewer to scratch a design into the black paint to reveal the hidden colors.

2. Look at the shapes below. Use your imagination to turn the shapes into sketches. While you doodle, think of ways to turn ordinary conversations into exciting conversations about Jesus.

PRAY

God, please help me recognize opportunities You give me to tell others about Jesus. Help me not be afraid to share my faith. *(Ask God to help you know the words to say when you tell others about Him.)*

71

WHAT A GIFT

All have sinned and fall short of the glory of God. They
are justified freely by his grace through the redemption
that is in Christ Jesus. *Romans 3:23–24*

Baylor and Caroline were eating a picnic in Baylor's backyard. Caroline swallowed her bite of sandwich and asked, "You're getting baptized on Sunday, right? Does that mean you'll be a Christian?"

Baylor shook her head, her eyes sparkling. "I'm already a Christian. Salvation is a gift! When I realized I was a sinner, I asked Jesus to forgive me. His forgiveness is what makes me a Christian. I'm getting baptized to show people what has happened—my sins are washed away, and I have new life with Jesus."

Caroline thought about what Baylor said. "So being a good person or going to church or even getting baptized doesn't make you a Christian?"

"Nope," Baylor said, smiling. "Confessing my sins and trusting Jesus does."

TODAY'S SPARK

Choose one of the following creative sparks to do today.

1. Draw a target on a piece of paper. Color the center red and print *JESUS* on it. Color the next ring yellow, and write things in it that are good things but not things that make you a Christian. Leave the last ring white, and list other things you do, good or bad. Toss a coin on the target. If the coin lands on *JESUS*, tell why He is the only way for salvation. If the coin lands anywhere else, tell why that thing is not what makes someone a Christian.

2. Many verses in Romans help people know about becoming a Christian. Use a highlighter to mark some of these verses in your Bible.

ROMANS 3:23

ROMANS 5:8

ROMANS 6:23

ROMANS 10:9-10

ROMANS 10:13

PRAY

Dear Jesus, thank You for the gift of salvation.
There is no other way back to God than through You.
*(Ask God to help friends you know understand
what becoming a Christian means.)*

72

POWERFUL PROOF

God proves his own love for us in that while we were
still sinners, Christ died for us. *Romans 5:8*

Have you ever been in the drive-through line, and when you approached the window, the car ahead of you had already paid for your food? This happened to a friend of mine! Even though she didn't know it, her food was being paid for. That's an exciting surprise, isn't it?

How much more exciting is it to realize that Jesus died for our sins before we were born, before we committed any sins? In fact, Jesus loved us before we were born. He loved us before we trusted in Him or asked Him to forgive our sins. Jesus proved His love by taking the punishment for our sins. We can't pay Jesus back for the amazing gift He has given us. But we can thank Him and tell others about Jesus' incredible love for them. Perhaps some of those people will be excited to hear the news too!

TODAY'S SPARK

Choose one of the following creative sparks to do today.

1. Do you know any songs that talk about Jesus loving us and dying for our sins? Ask a parent to help you create a playlist and listen to them together.

2. Cut out three identical size hearts. Write a part of Romans 5:8 on each heart. Fold the hearts to make a vertical crease down the middle of each heart. Use glue sticks to put glue on the back of all three hearts. To assemble, attach the back of one-half of heart number one to the matching half of heart number two. Do the same thing to attach heart number two to heart number three. Put a loop of yarn along the seam before attaching heart number three to heart number one. Hang by the loop so that the heart spins.

PRAY

Jesus, You loved me even before I knew about You. You died for my sins long before I committed them. Thank You for redeeming Me. *(Ask Jesus to give you boldness to tell others you believe in Him.)*

73

OUR PART

If you confess with your mouth, "Jesus is Lord,"
and believe in your heart that God raised him from
the dead, you will be saved. *Romans 10:9*

Lucas was helping his mom put mulch around the flowerbeds. "I've been thinking, and I'm a little confused about something."

"What's confusing, honey?" Mom replied while she worked.

"Well, I know salvation is God's gift. We can't earn it, and Jesus died for our sins long before I was born. So how come everyone isn't automatically a Christian?" Lucas asked.

Mom looked up and answered, "I see why that's confusing. Well, God didn't make us robots that He could control. It's not like what you get to do with the characters in your video games. We are made in God's image, but at the same time, we are responsible for our own choices. In faith, we admit that we need God's forgiveness and then tell others about what we've experienced with Him!"

"I see," said Lucas, emptying the mulch bag. "So God offers the gift through Jesus, but we still have to accept it. That's what makes us human."

TODAY'S SPARK

Choose one of the following creative sparks to do today.

1. Create a painting to remind you that Jesus is Lord. Your design might be a cross or an empty tomb or a heart. Sketch your design lightly with pencil, then go over the image with white crayon. Use watercolors to color in the spaces, and while the paint is wet, sprinkle a few grains of salt to create a raised texture.

2. Like Lucas, do you have questions about God? Start a journal with your questions, and find an adult you feel comfortable talking about these things with.

PRAY

Jesus, thank You for understanding my questions
and sometimes giving me the answers through
other people. Help me to trust You always. *(Ask Jesus to give
You answers and understanding when you read the Bible.)*

GOD'S AMAZING REDEMPTION

If anyone is in Christ, he is a new creation; the old has passed
away, and see, the new has come! *2 Corinthians 5:17*

Saige emptied the bag into the recycling bin. "I wonder what these plastic bottles will be turned into," she asked her uncle Bud.

"I'm not sure, but it's nice to think they can be reused rather than just dumped in a landfill somewhere," Uncle Bud answered as they headed back inside.

"So when we become Christians, are we kind of recycled too?" Saige asked.

Uncle Bud thought for a moment and then replied, "You know, Saige, it's even better than that. We aren't just formed into something else. We become brand-new from the inside, from our souls. Before, we didn't care about obeying God, but now we want to. That affects our choices and how we think about life—it changes everything! We become new creations, and God promises that when we are in heaven, we'll have new bodies too!"

"Oh, that sounds nice," said Saige. "I'm tired of my allergies."

"I hear you," said Uncle Bud. "This old body has lots of aches and pains. I'm ready for my new one!"

Choose one of the following creative sparks to do today.

1. Butterflies are a good example of *transformation* or becoming new. Fold a piece of paper in half and open it back up. On one half of the paper, draw half a butterfly with a black oil pastel. Fold the paper back together and rub, pressing hard, with the handle of a pair of scissors. Open the paper and use the oil pastel to trace the faint lines you see. Color the butterfly with vibrant colors.

2. In your journal, write down some of your sins. Cover those sins with sticky notes and write out verses about God's forgiveness on the sticky notes: Ephesians 2:8; Psalm 103:12; 1 John 1:9; Psalm 86:5; and 2 Corinthians 5:17.

PRAY

God, thank You that I don't have to fix myself. You promise to make me a new creation. *(Ask God to help you know the things He wants you to change or improve.)*

75

JESUS PAID IT ALL

In Christ, God was reconciling
the world to himself. *2 Corinthians 5:19*

What does *reconcile* mean? If you have a bank account, it means the amounts are correct and things are paid. Our sin is like a huge debt owed to God, but Jesus paid the whole debt. God provided so that we could be completely reconciled to Him.

One Sunday in 1865, Elvina Hall was sitting in the choir at her church, and her mind began to wander. She thought about how people needed salvation and what Jesus had done to pay for our salvation. Words began to come to her, and she quickly wrote them down on a blank page in her songbook. After church, she showed the words to the pastor. The pastor knew of a tune that the church organist, John Grape, had recently written. The words and the tune were a perfect fit. Many hymn (song) books have their song, "Jesus Paid It All."

Have you ever heard the song? These are the lyrics of the chorus:

Jesus paid it all, All to Him I owe;
Sin had left a crimson stain, He washed it white as snow.

TODAY'S SPARK

Choose one of the following creative sparks to do today.

1. Elvina Hall was thinking about what Jesus did, and she wrote down the words to "Jesus Paid It All." Spend a few moments thinking about what Jesus did for you, then write it down. You might write phrases, sentences, a poem, or a song. Let the words flow out of you as they cross your mind. Try to use the word *reconcile* if you can.

2. Make a maze by gluing various lengths of drinking straws to a paper plate or box lid. Make sure there is only one solution from *Start* to *Finish*. When you're done, write along the path: "Jesus is the only way to salvation."

PRAY

God, thank You for reconciling us to Yourself. (*Spend time looking up the writers of your favorite worship songs. Thank God for people like Elvina who write songs that help us remember what Jesus did.*)

76

AMBASSADORS

We are ambassadors for Christ, since God is making his appeal through us. We plead on Christ's behalf, "Be reconciled to God." *2 Corinthians 5:20*

The house smelled so good. Mom and Mimi had been cooking all day because Uncle Clayton was visiting. Uncle Clayton was an ambassador, so he lived in a country far away.

On his last visit, Uncle Clayton had explained that an ambassador connects two groups of people. He lived in an assigned country while representing his own country.

In church the day before, Hudson had heard the pastor say Christians were ambassadors for Christ. Sitting at the kitchen table, he asked Mom and Mimi what that meant.

"Great question," said Mimi as she stirred the soup. "Christians represent Jesus as we live among people who don't know Him. We tell our neighbors, friends, and coworkers what it's like to love Jesus. As His ambassadors, we represent His kingdom, a spiritual kingdom."

"That's right," said Mom. "Now some people, like missionaries, move to other places to tell people about Jesus. But all Christians can be ambassadors wherever we are!"

TODAY'S SPARK

Choose one of the following creative sparks to do today.

1. Make up a rap that includes the word *ambassadors*. What other words can you use in the rap as reminders that we are ambassadors for Christ?

2. Do you know someone who is sick or lonely? Make a sunshine basket as an ambassador for Jesus. Fill the basket with yellow tissue paper and yellow goodies (cookies, candy, flowers, lip balm) since yellow can remind people of happiness. Add a note that says God loves them and you are praying for them.

PRAY

God, help me to be Your ambassador right where I am. Show me who needs to see the love You have put in my heart. *(Ask God to give you creativity in the ways you can share His love with people around you.)*

77

ADOPTED

> When the time came to completion, God sent his Son, born of a woman, born under the law, to redeem those under the law, so that we might receive adoption as sons. *Galatians 4:4–5*

Mom and Riley turned the pages of the photo album and talked about the day Riley was adopted. Riley had been so little that she couldn't remember the day. But she loved to hear Mom tell the story. Mom always cried, explaining they were happy tears.

"You have another day to celebrate now," Mom said. "The day you trusted Jesus as your Savior is the day you were adopted into God's family." Mom opened her Bible and read Galatians 4:4–5 to Riley.

Riley's smile grew even bigger. "Adopted as sons and daughters? That means we both are adopted into God's family, Mom, because we are both Christians!" Riley noticed another tear roll down her mom's cheek. "Why are you crying now, Mom?"

"These are extra happy tears!" Mom said, smiling. "Because of what you just said."

TODAY'S SPARK

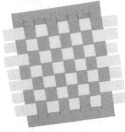

Choose one of the following creative sparks to do today.

1. Try paper weaving as a reminder that when you become a Christian, you are woven into God's family. Take two different colored pieces of paper the same size. Cut slits the same width in the first paper but stop about an inch from the end; don't cut all the way through. Cut the other paper into strips the same width as the first paper's strips. Alternate over-under weaving with the second color.

2. As a family, draw portraits: Give everyone in your family a sheet of paper and a marker. Call out one part of a face to draw (such as eyes, nose, ear, hair, etc.). Pass all the papers to the right and call out another facial feature. Keep passing until everyone has drawn on each portrait.

PRAY

God, thank You that believers are part of Your forever family. *(Thank God for the people in your earthly family and, if you have trusted Jesus as Savior, your spiritual family.)*

78

COMPLETE FORGIVENESS

In him we have redemption through his blood, the forgiveness of our trespasses, according to the riches of his grace. *Ephesians 1:7*

Kelsey was quiet after Sunday brunch. She was thinking about the communion service or, as Dad called it, the Lord's Supper.

"Dad," said Kelsey, "we talk about blood a lot when we talk about Jesus. The cup of juice reminds us of the blood Jesus shed. We sing songs about the blood. Why is His blood so important?"

Dad nodded. "Well, Jesus didn't *just* die; He became the final sacrifice for our sins." Dad picked up His Bible, opened it to Hebrews 10:11–12, and read, "Every priest stands day after day ministering and offering the same sacrifices time after time, which can never take away sins. But this man [Jesus], after offering one sacrifice for sins forever, sat down at the right hand of God."

"Our sin demands a sacrifice," said Dad. "In the Old Testament, people sacrificed animals, but there was always a need for more. In the New Testament, Jesus became the full and final sacrifice. During communion, we worship Him for that, never forgetting how He showed His love for us when He died on the cross."

TODAY'S SPARK

Choose one of the following creative sparks to do today.

1. In your journal, write a letter to yourself as a reminder of the complete forgiveness Jesus gives through His full and final sacrifice.

2. Create a mini poster by decorating with "fork flowers." Dip a plastic fork in paint and press it onto paper to make flower petals in a flower shape. Add real stems, leaves, and grass to the poster. Write Bible verses on the paper about God's love for people.

PRAY

Jesus, thank You for being willing to be our sacrifice and take the punishment for all our sins. I love You! *(Ask Jesus to help you always remember what He has done for you.)*

79

GOD'S GIFT

You are saved by grace through faith, and this is not from yourselves; it is God's gift—not from works, so that no one can boast. *Ephesians 2:8–9*

Baleigh invited her friend Renee to Bible class every Wednesday night. One night, Renee said, "At church, the leaders talk a lot about being a Christian, but I'm not sure how. Do you have to be a good person or read the whole Bible first?"

Baleigh smiled. "There's nothing we can *do* to become a Christian. If we could, we'd just boast about what we had done."

Renee nodded. "That's true!" Her eyebrows furrowed. "But then, what hope do I have?"

"That's just it. Our hope is in God only. He sent Jesus to take all our punishment. When we turn to Jesus and confess our sins, He offers the free gift of forgiveness, and we receive it through faith. *Faith* is trusting something because God says it's true. God says we're saved through faith."

"Well, I have faith," said Renee. "I believe Jesus loves me and died for my sins. I want to follow Him right now." The girls hugged and prayed together. It was a moment to celebrate!

TODAY'S SPARK

Choose one of the following creative sparks to do today.

1. Make your own wrapping paper. Start with a roll of white art paper and some markers or stamps and inkpads. Decorate the paper with phrases about Jesus' love. Use the paper to wrap birthday gifts for friends.

2. Write a thank-you note to God that includes everything you know about becoming a Christian. Include Scriptures if that helps remind you of the truth.

PRAY

God, thank You for the gift of forgiveness through Jesus. Thank You that Your plan for redeeming us is way better than the one we would have come up with. *(Talk with God about what His forgiveness means to you.)*

80

FAITHFUL REDEEMER

If we confess our sins, he is faithful and righteous to forgive us our sins and to cleanse us from all unrighteousness. *1 John 1:9*

Luke climbed into the front seat when his after-school detention was over. Mom silently started the truck and headed home.

Finally Luke said, "I messed up again and said some things I shouldn't have to Mr. Allen."

"Did you apologize?" Mom asked. Luke nodded.

"That's good," Mom said. "You'll still have consequences, but at least you told Mr. Allen you were sorry."

"I thought once I became a Christian, I wouldn't do wrong things anymore," Luke sighed. "But I still mess up. Do I have to ask Jesus to forgive me again?"

Mom pulled in the driveway and faced Luke. "Becoming a Christian isn't an automatic fix," she said. "As humans, we still have a sin nature. You trusted Jesus as your Savior, but to keep that relationship strong, you still ask for forgiveness when you sin. Think of it like this: you are my son and always will be, but when you ask me for forgiveness, it makes things better between us. It's the same with Jesus . . . and probably Mr. Allen."

Choose one of the following creative sparks to do today.

1. Try to draw what your relationship with Jesus feels like—the good, the bad, and the ugly. Don't worry if the image is abstract.

2. Find a quiet place to sit and think about all that Jesus means to you. Sing a favorite song of praise to worship Him.

PRAY

Jesus, thank You for not turning Your back on me when I mess up. Thank You for Your promise of forgiveness. *(Talk to Jesus about things you need forgiveness for, or thank Him for forgiveness He has already given you.)*

81

THE HOLY SPIRIT

The earth was formless and empty, darkness covered the surface of the watery depths, and the Spirit of God was hovering over the surface of the waters. *Genesis 1:2*

Are you ever confused about how God the Father, Jesus the Son, and the Holy Spirit can all be God? It's okay to be confused. It makes sense that we cannot understand everything about God. But the Bible shows us in different places that the Trinity (God being one God and three persons at the same time) is real.

- At Creation: Genesis 1 says that when God the Father created the world, the Spirit of God was there, hovering over the waters. Then John 1 tells us that Jesus was there, too, and everything in creation was created through Him.
- During Jesus' baptism: In Matthew 3, God the Father spoke from heaven declaring Jesus was His Son, and the Holy Spirit descended in the form of a dove.

The one true God in three persons—Father, Son, and Holy Spirit—has been and always will be the God who created the world, provided a way to be saved, and loves us. He is ruling over creation, redeeming sinners to Himself, and He is always with us.

TODAY'S SPARK

Choose one of the following creative sparks to do today.

1. Drop a small puddle of brown paint near the bottom of a piece of paper. Blow slowly through a drinking straw onto the paint, pushing the paint up and in various directions. It should resemble a tree. After it dries, add either real or painted leaves. Think about how God's Spirit moved across the surface of the waters before Creation.

2. Make a window aquarium. Cut a large rectangle from blue cellophane and fold it in half. Insert pictures of fish that you cut out or draw. Glue in place. Add real plants, artificial plants, or drawings of plants so that it looks like an aquarium. Seal the three open sides with black duct tape. Attach to a window.

PRAY

God, because You are God, You are bigger than we can comprehend, but I believe in You. Thank You for creating me, saving me, and loving me. *(Ask God to help your faith grow as you learn more about Him.)*

82

THE HOLY SPIRIT GUIDES US

The Spirit of the Lord God is on me, because the Lord has anointed me to bring good news to the poor. He has sent me to heal the brokenhearted, to proclaim liberty to the captives and freedom to the prisoners. Isaiah 61:1

The Holy Spirit is sometimes called "the Spirit of the Lord God" or "the Spirit of God" in the Old Testament. We know that the Holy Spirit was working and guiding people in the Old Testament, especially the prophets who shared God's messages with the people.

Isaiah is one of the prophets who wrote about things that God revealed to him. The words in Isaiah 61:1–2 are words Jesus would later read in His hometown synagogue at Nazareth (Luke 4:18–19). As He read them, Jesus was telling the people He Himself had come to fulfill those words—to proclaim good news and freedom, and to heal.

God knew everything that would happen in the future because He is always in control. The Holy Spirit guided the authors of the Bible, like Isaiah during Old Testament times, to write God's messages down. The Holy Spirit is still our guide today as we study the Bible and learn more about the good news God promised through Jesus.

TODAY'S SPARK

Choose one of the following creative sparks to do today.

1. Try setting a pattern of dominos in a design so that they fall down consecutively when the first one is pushed over. Think about how God is in control of much more than dominos—He knows how everything comes together and works together in the world. He knows what the future holds.

2. When Jesus recited Isaiah 61, He said He had come to heal the brokenhearted. Is there something around your house that needs fixing? Do you have the tools to fix it? If you need adult supervision, ask someone; then fix what is currently broken.

PRAY

God, thank You for the Holy Spirit who guided the authors of the Bible and guides us today as we study it. *(Ask God's Spirit to help you learn more as you read and study your Bible.)*

83

THE PROMISED HELPER

"I will ask the Father, and he will give you another Counselor to be with you forever." *John 14:16*

Jesus spent three years with His disciples teaching them about and modeling the kingdom of heaven. What a blessing it must have been to sit with Jesus around a campfire, at a mealtime, or walking along the road as He spoke! The disciples loved talking with Jesus and listening to His answers to their questions.

But Jesus knew that He would not always be physically with His disciples on earth. So He promised to send the Holy Spirit, who would be with each of them, no matter where they were or what they were going through.

We have never seen Jesus in person, but as Christians, we have the blessing of the Holy Spirit living inside of us. Jesus actually said it is better that way (John 16:7). The Holy Spirit helps us know about God and understand His Word. Jesus also said that those who have not seen Him yet still believe in Him are blessed (John 20:29). That's us!

TODAY'S SPARK

Choose one of the following creative sparks to do today.

1. Pretend you are one of the disciples. Write what you think it would have been like to spend time in person with Jesus. Make sure to include details about sight, smell, taste, touch, and sound.

2. Make a comfort square to share with someone having a hard time or not feeling well. Cut a square of fleece material and fringe the edges with scissors. Remember that, like the Holy Spirit comforts us, we can comfort others.

PRAY

Jesus, thank You for the blessing of the Holy Spirit, our Counselor and Comforter. Help me to listen to Him as I would listen to You. *(Ask the Holy Spirit to guide you as you learn more about Jesus.)*

84

HE WILL BE WITH YOU

"He is the Spirit of truth. The world is unable to receive him because it doesn't see him or know him. But you do know him, because he remains with you and will be in you." *John 14:17*

Mom zipped up the lunch box and handed it to Abigail. She could tell Abigail was deep in thought. "What are you thinking about so seriously?" Mom asked.

"We start classes for the new semester at school today. I have to find new rooms and get used to new teachers. I'm worried it will be hard and I won't like it," Abigail admitted.

Mom gave Abigail a hug. "Do you remember what we read last night about the Holy Spirit? You trusted Jesus as your Savior, and that means the Holy Spirit is in you and *remains* with you. That means He stays with you all the time, even at school. You are never alone."

Abigail looked down at her lap. "I guess I figured God wouldn't care about little things like school schedules. But He's with me and can help me through anything, even this!" This made her look up and smile.

TODAY'S SPARK

Choose one of the following creative sparks to do today.

1. Walk around your house and think up a sentence to say to the rhythm of your steps. You might repeat, "God is with me. God is with me." Try it for several minutes. Notice if it comes back to you later this week, just when you need it.

2. Make a windsock. Cut the bottom out of a disposable plastic cup. Punch several holes and tie ribbons to the mouth end of the cup. Punch two holes and tie a loop of cord for a hanger through the open bottom end of the cup. Hang the windsock by the hanger outside. You can't see the wind, but you see what it does when the cup and ribbons move. Even though you can't see the Holy Spirit, you know what He is doing.

PRAY

God, sometimes I get worried or afraid.
When that feeling comes, help me remember
You are always with me. *(Thank the Holy Spirit, who is
there to comfort you, even though you can't see Him.)*

85

HE WILL TEACH YOU

The Counselor, the Holy Spirit, whom the Father will send in my name, will teach you all things and remind you of everything I have told you. *John 14:26*

Christopher found Aunt Isabel outside in the swing, reading her Bible. She looked up when he sat down next to her. "I've tried reading the Bible," Christopher said. "But there's so much I don't understand. Maybe it's because I'm too young. How long did it take you to understand the Bible?"

Aunt Isabel laughed. "Oh, honey, I'm still learning! I don't understand everything in the Bible. But I have learned a couple of important things: First, I make it a daily habit to read from God's Word. Even when I have more questions than answers, I know reading my Bible helps me focus on God first. Second, I've learned to trust the Holy Spirit. Jesus promised the Holy Spirit would teach us what we need to know."

"Oh," said Christopher thoughtfully. "So it's okay if I don't understand everything every time? The Holy Spirit will help me know what I need to know?" Aunt Isabel answered yes with a hug and a big smile.

TODAY'S SPARK

Choose one of the following creative sparks to do today.

1. If you've already made a quiet-time box, consider decorating it more with references to your favorite Bible passages. Write out some of those verses, and slide them in your box to meditate on during your next quiet time.

2. The Holy Spirit helps us understand God's Word. Write the word *UNDERSTAND* vertically on a piece of paper and create an acrostic with words or phrases that describe the Holy Spirit.

PRAY

God, thank You for the Holy Spirit, who teaches us as we study Your Word. *(Ask God to help you find time every day to read your Bible.)*

86

HE WILL HELP YOU UNDERSTAND

"When the Counselor comes, the one I will send to you from the Father—the Spirit of truth who proceeds from the Father—he will testify about me." *John 15:26*

Kyndall watched her older sister, Donna, packing her suitcase. Donna and their church youth group were going on a mission trip. Kyndall watched as Donna carefully checked the case that held her Bible, some highlighters and pens, and a notebook. "Do you have to do homework on your trip?" Kyndall asked.

"These are for my Bible study times. We'll have a quiet time every morning to read our Bibles and pray before we start our days," Donna explained.

"How do you know the things you read in the Bible are true?" Kyndall asked.

Donna thought a minute. "Jesus said that the Holy Spirit would help us know the truth. He helps us know the evidence about Jesus is real. The more I read my Bible and talk to other people who believe in Jesus, the more I understand. You will too. Keep reading your Bible and praying."

TODAY'S SPARK

Choose one of the following creative sparks to do today.

1. Decorate a pencil cup to keep your highlighters and pens together by your quiet-time box. Make sure to put a favorite pen or highlighter in the cup!

2. As you learn about the Holy Spirit and how He works, you may have questions. Write your questions in your journal. As time goes on and you discover answers, write them in your journal too.

PRAY

God, Your plan is perfect. Thank You that Your plan included sending the Holy Spirit, who helps us understand the truth about Jesus. *(Talk to God about some of the things you are learning about the Holy Spirit.)*

87

HE WILL SHOW YOU THE TRUTH

"When the Spirit of truth comes, he will guide you into all the truth. For he will not speak on his own, but he will speak whatever he hears. He will also declare to you what is to come." John 16:13

John, one of Jesus' original twelve disciples, wrote five books that we have in the New Testament. At one point, John said that if everything Jesus did had been recorded, the world could not even hold all the books (John 21:25).

Jesus taught His disciples many things, but as the time of Jesus' death drew near, He knew there wasn't time to teach them everything. In John 16:12, He said, "I still have many things to tell you, but you can't bear them now." Then He promised that the Spirit of truth, the Holy Spirit, would come and guide His disciples.

The guidance of the Holy Spirit is from God. The Holy Spirit is the Spirit of truth for us today too (Ephesians 1:13–14). God sent the Holy Spirit to guide us and help us know the truth. With His help, we can know Jesus more.

TODAY'S SPARK

Choose one of the following creative sparks to do today.

1. Make a kazoo with an empty paper towel tube, wax paper, and a rubber band. Cut the tube in half, then cut a square of wax paper to fit over one end of the tube. Secure with a rubber band. Hum or sing through the open end of the tube. Sing a praise song about the Holy Spirit.

2. John said if everything Jesus did were recorded, the whole world could not contain the books. Make your own book of facts, illustrations, and memories of what God has done for you. Share your book with someone.

PRAY

God, You don't expect me to know everything. That's why You gave us the Holy Spirit. *(Thank God for the Holy Spirit, who helps Christians know how to follow God.)*

88

THE HOLY SPIRIT'S PURPOSE

"You will receive power when the Holy Spirit has come on you, and you will be my witnesses in Jerusalem, in all Judea and Samaria, and to the ends of the earth." *Acts 1:8*

Kaden rolled his eyes as his little brother Charlie raced into the room with a towel tied around his neck like a superhero cape. Charlie screeched to a halt, made muscle arms, and shouted, "I have the power!" before sprinting off.

Kaden went back to the Bible verse card from Kids Club. He was supposed to have it memorized by tonight's meeting. *"You will receive power." That's interesting.* Kaden thought. *God has promised us power, and if God promised it, then it's real power. It's not pretend like Charlie thinks he has.* Then Kaden prayed, *God, what kind of power do You give?*

As Kaden memorized Acts 1:8, he began to understand that God's power helps people do supernatural spiritual things, like loving their enemies, forgiving those who sin against them, and telling people about Jesus wherever they go.

TODAY'S SPARK

Choose one of the following creative sparks to do today.

1. Try making a boat (or raft) using only plastic drinking straws and masking tape. Put several straws side by side to make the floor of the raft first. Test your raft to see if it floats, and then test it to see how heavy of a load it can support. Now think about the places you might travel to one day, whether by boat or car or plane. Remember that Jesus said we are to be witnesses about Him wherever we go!

2. Use sidewalk chalk to write a Bible verse or create a message on your sidewalk about God. Make it large enough so that people who pass by can see it.

PRAY

God, thank You for giving me the Holy Spirit so I have supernatural power to tell others of Your great love! *(Thank God for the Holy Spirit, who empowers you to be a witness for God.)*

89

GOD'S TIMING, PART 1

"Look, I am sending you what my Father promised. As for you, stay in the city until you are empowered from on high." *Luke 24:49*

Harper listened with excitement as her cousin, Victoria, told her about the Bible story she had heard at church. "Then, while the disciples watched," Victoria shared with enthusiasm, "Jesus went straight up to heaven in a cloud!"

"Really?" Harper exclaimed. "What did the disciples do next?"

Victoria continued, "Jesus told them to go back to town and wait for a special Helper who would give them the power to do what God had planned for them to do. Jesus had explained He had to go back to heaven, but the Holy Spirit would come to help them. So the disciples just waited."

"That must have been so hard," said Harper.

"I know! But ten days later, the Holy Spirit came to empower the disciples to tell the good news, and it wasn't what anyone expected."

Choose one of the following creative sparks to do today.

1. Make a photo journal of clouds this week. Take a picture of the clouds every day, possibly multiple times a day. Save them in a digital file. At the end of the week, review all your photos and praise Jesus for ascending into heaven.

2. Pretend you could go back in time. Write a story based on Luke 24:49–53 as if you had been there, witnessing Jesus be taken into heaven.

PRAY

God, sometimes, like the disciples, we have to wait for Your promise to come true. Your timing is always perfect. *(Ask God to help you trust Him when you are waiting for an answer to your prayers.)*

90

GOD'S TIMING, PART 2

They were all filled with the Holy Spirit and began to speak in different tongues, as the Spirit enabled them. *Acts 2:4*

Victoria had been telling her cousin, Harper, about the things that happened just ten days after Jesus returned to heaven.

"What does *filled with the Holy Spirit* mean?" Harper asked.

"It means that the Holy Spirit gave the disciples the power to do more than they could do on their own," Victoria explained. "On the day of Pentecost, they were gathered in a room, waiting, just like Jesus told them to. Suddenly they heard a sound of a mighty wind, and something that looked like flames hovered over their heads. At the time, Jerusalem was filled with people from many countries celebrating Pentecost. Well, the Holy Spirit gave the disciples the ability to speak good news about Jesus in their different languages!"

"That's awesome," said Harper. "Definitely supernatural."

"True, but supernatural with a purpose," continued Victoria. "There's one thing the Holy Spirit always does: He helps us understand who Jesus is and why we need Him to be our Savior."

TODAY'S SPARK

Choose one of the following creative sparks to do today.

1. Go on a sound scavenger hunt. Draw a grid of nine or twelve squares. Fill in each square with a sound you might hear (examples: bird singing, wind blowing, siren blaring). Take a walk outside and mark off each sound you hear. Continue your scavenger hunt throughout the week. Remember that the disciples heard the sound of rushing wind on Pentecost.

2. Have you ever spoken in Pig Latin? Look up the rules, which are fairly simple, and try speaking only in Pig Latin for the evening.

PRAY

God, thank You for the Holy Spirit who gives me the courage to tell others about Jesus. *(Ask God to give you the supernatural strength to talk to others about Him.)*

91

PROOF OF THE HOLY SPIRIT

Since he [Jesus] has been exalted to the right hand of God and has received from the Father the promised Holy Spirit, he has poured out what you both see and hear. *Acts 2:33*

The disciples waited in Jerusalem just like Jesus told them to. Jews from many countries had come to Jerusalem to celebrate a special feast. On the day of Pentecost, the Holy Spirit came and empowered them to preach the good news in many languages so that all the people visiting for the festival could hear and understand. You can read about the event in Acts chapter 2.

Peter's sermon begins at verse 14. Peter quoted Scripture from the prophets and told about events the people had recently witnessed. He talked about Jesus' ministry and His death and resurrection. Peter explained that the things people were seeing in that moment were the evidence that the Holy Spirit had come, just as Jesus had promised. After that, three thousand people believed in Jesus!

TODAY'S SPARK

Choose one of the following creative sparks to do today.

1. Think about all the ways you can multiply two numbers to equal three thousand. When you're done, worship God for saving three thousand people in one day after Peter's sermon.

2. Cut a paper plate into a spiral. Along the spiral, write things you know about Jesus or the Holy Spirit. Attach a piece of yarn to the end of the spiral, and hang it, so it can move in the breeze.

PRAY

God, You have given us proof that You are who You say You are. By Your power and Your power alone are people saved. *(Ask the Holy Spirit to be your Helper when telling others about Jesus.)*

92

"WE ARE WITNESSES"

"We are witnesses of these things, and so is the Holy Spirit whom God has given to those who obey him." *Acts 5:32*

After the excitement on the day of Pentecost, you might think everything was great for the original disciples, who were often called *apostles*. Peter and the other apostles kept preaching about Jesus, but it angered the Sanhedrin, or the highest Jewish officials, led by the high priest. They arrested the apostles and put them in jail.

When Peter and the other apostles were brought before the Sanhedrin, the high priest asked why they were teaching in the name of Jesus when they had been ordered to stop. The apostles replied they had to obey God rather than men (Acts 5:28–29). They had a new purpose in life now. They couldn't stop talking about Jesus and His resurrection.

The apostles knew what was true about Jesus because they were firsthand witnesses (they had actually seen the risen Jesus). But it was the Holy Spirit who empowered them—in the face of danger—to speak boldly about Jesus.

TODAY'S SPARK

Choose one of the following creative sparks to do today.

1. Each of the shapes below indicates an action to create a rhythm. Try the rhythm in the design. Next, copy the shapes onto individual index cards. Rearrange them to create your own rhythm. Put words about the apostles to your rhythm.

2. What is a creative passion you have that you can't stop talking about, learning about, or doing? How might you use that passion to tell others about Jesus? Write down your ideas.

PRAY

God, please help Christians around the world who face danger because they love You. *(Thank God for the Holy Spirit, who helps us have courage to speak up for what we know about Jesus and who helps us know what to say.)*

93

GOD'S FAMILY CONNECTION

All those led by God's Spirit are God's sons. *Romans 8:14*

Tyler and his mom were packing their lunches for school and work. Tyler grabbed a piece of fruit and said, "I had a weird thing happen yesterday."

"Oh, what was that?" Mom asked as she dropped sandwiches in both their bags.

"There was this new kid in class," Tyler explained. "When we went to lunch, I had a feeling that I should ask him to sit with us. He seemed kind of nervous and relieved at the same time."

Mom smiled. "The Holy Spirit often nudges us to do the things that would honor God. It sounds like you were willing to follow that nudge. Being kind to a new kid would definitely be something that lines up with what God wants us to do."

Tyler grabbed his lunch. "Yeah," he said. "I'm going to ask him to join us again today."

TODAY'S SPARK

Choose one of the following creative sparks to do today.

1. Do you have a hobby? Maybe you like to construct sculptures, read, or play the piano. Is there someone else who might enjoy doing that hobby with you? Spend some time pondering the possibilities.

2. Make a prayer list on index cards. Write each person's name on a separate card, and list ways you can pray for them. Start with just one or two people, and add more as the Holy Spirit leads you to.

PRAY

God, help me know when the Holy Spirit is leading
me to follow Your will. I want to honor You with my life.
*(Thank God for the reminder that being led by the
Holy Spirit is proof we are His sons and daughters.)*

94

ASSURANCE

The Spirit himself testifies together with our spirit that we are God's children. *Romans 8:16*

I wish I could pray like Grandpa," Mary Ella said on the way home.

"What do you mean?" asked Mom.

"It seems like Grandpa is so close to God when he prays; it's like he's talking to a friend," said Mary Ella.

"Grandpa has been a Christian for a long time, and he takes his relationship with God seriously. He knows prayer is talking to God, so he is comfortable talking to Him like a friend. The more you pray, the more you will realize God hears and cares about everything you say or think."

"That makes sense," said Mary Ella.

"That's one way the Holy Spirit helps us know we are God's children," Mom explained. "We begin to recognize that connection to God, especially when we pray."

TODAY'S SPARK

Choose one of the following creative sparks to do today.

1. Make a prayer calendar for the next month. Instead of writing in a journal, write down your prayer request inside each calendar day. The following month, check back in on the calendar and notice what prayers God has already answered.

2. Create thumbprint art by pressing your thumb on an inkpad and making a design on paper. Think about how each human has a unique thumbprint, and each human is invited to have their own relationship with God.

PRAY

Thank You, God, that the Holy Spirit reminds us
we are Your children, so we can always talk to You!
*(If there is something you have kept from
God in prayer, bring it to Him now.)*

95

THE HOLY SPIRIT PRAYS FOR US

The Spirit also helps us in our weakness, because we do not know what to pray for as we should, but the Spirit himself intercedes for us with unspoken groanings. *Romans 8:26*

Mr. Franks wrote the prayer requests on the board before Bible study time. Carson felt more depressed as more names were added. So many people were sick or hurting.

Later, Carson told Mr. Franks, "I try to pray for the people on our prayer list, but sometimes it feels like all I can say is, 'Please help Joe's friend or heal Mrs. Brooks.' I care about everyone, but I feel pretty helpless."

"God knows your heart," Mr. Franks said reassuringly. "More than that, God promised the Holy Spirit would pray for us when we are too weak to pray. God doesn't need us to tell Him what to do—that's not what prayer is. He simply wants us to bring our concerns to Him however we can."

"So you're saying I don't always have to have the right words? The Holy Spirit can speak for me?" asked Carson, eyes bright. "That makes my spirit feel stronger already."

TODAY'S SPARK

Choose one of the following creative sparks to do today.

1. In your prayer journal, list things you are not sure how to pray about—maybe you don't know what to ask, or you don't have the words. Print "Trust God" at the top to remind you of what prayer is.

2. Take a prayer walk around where you live. Pray for the people you know are in need and the people you don't know much about.

PRAY

Thank You, God, that our specific words are not important but what's in our hearts is. *(If there's anything you had a hard time praying about recently, ask the Holy Spirit to pray on your behalf.)*

96

THE HOLY SPIRIT GIVES US HOPE

May the God of hope fill you with all joy and peace as you believe so that you may overflow with hope by the power of the Holy Spirit. Romans 15:13

Audrey saw Mrs. Gladys limp into church using her walker and carefully sit down at the end of the row. Mrs. Gladys had the sweetest smile on her face and greeted everyone with joy in her voice. Audrey knew Mrs. Gladys had experienced difficulties in life—her husband dying recently and her only son moving overseas—and that her health was not good.

Audrey slid down to where Mrs. Gladys was sitting. "Oh, hello, Audrey. I'm so glad to see you today," Mrs. Gladys said, giving Audrey a hug.

"How are you always so happy?" Audrey blurted out. "It looks like you are having a hard time walking today, and I know you are sad about things."

"Oh, I do have a lot of sadness, and this weather has my old knees in bad shape. But just look at my blessings!" Mrs. Gladys said, smiling, "I'm worshiping my Savior today, and I get to do it here with you. God fills my heart with hope, so I am happy."

TODAY'S SPARK

Choose one of the following creative sparks to do today.

1. Turn on some praise music. Have fun twirling around or using scarves or ribbons to swirl as you dance. Thank God for the ability to move and groove.

2. Design a "Thinking of You" card. Print Romans 15:13 on a card, and add a note of encouragement to send to someone you know who needs a lift.

PRAY

God, thank You for the hope we have in You.
(Talk to God about the feelings of joy and peace you have when you think about His love for you.)

97

THE HOLY SPIRIT SHOWS US TRUTH

God has revealed these things to us by the Spirit, since the Spirit searches everything, even the depths of God. *1 Corinthians 2:10*

Have you ever heard someone say, "I've never noticed that in the Bible before!" Chances are they have read the passage before, but it didn't catch their attention the first time.

Reading the Bible is exciting because the Holy Spirit points things out as we grow in our faith. Sometimes a part of a verse will stick in your thoughts, and you can't stop thinking about it. Sometimes you'll notice the same verse over and over as you read different devotionals, attend church, or do Bible studies. Other times, something in the Bible you've been confused about for years will suddenly make sense.

These are some of the ways the Holy Spirit guides us to the truth of God. If anyone says they understand *everything* in the Bible, they are wrong. Even the best Bible scholars readily admit the more they read, the more they realize how much they don't know!

TODAY'S SPARK

Choose one of the following creative sparks to do today.

1. Cut a strip of felt the size you prefer for a bookmark. Grab a needle, thread, sequins, and small beads. Thread the needle. Push the needle up through the felt, but don't pull it all the way through. Slide a sequin onto the needle. Slide a bead on top of the sequin, then finish pulling the needle through the felt, but don't pull the thread all the way. Push the needle back through the hole in the sequin and through the felt. Tie the two ends of thread together, and snip the ends. Add as many sequins as you like. Use as a bookmark in your Bible.

2. Make a simpler bookmark by cutting the corner off an envelope to make a closed triangle shape. The two straight sides should be about two inches long. Decorate the envelope corner with stickers or markers. Slip the envelope corner over the corner of your Bible page to hold your place.

PRAY

God, help me make reading my Bible a priority.
Thank You that I don't have to understand
everything right away to be a Christian. *(Ask God
to bless the time you spend reading His Word.)*

98

THE HOLY SPIRIT EMPOWERS US

We also speak these things, not in words taught by human wisdom, but in those taught by the Spirit, explaining spiritual things to spiritual people. *1 Corinthians 2:13*

Mason climbed into the back seat. His older brother, Noah, was driving his buddy and Mason to the soccer field. Mason listened while Noah talked with his friend, answering the questions the friend had about what being a Christian really meant.

Later, Mason asked Noah, "How did you know what to say when you were talking with your friend? I didn't know you knew all that stuff."

Noah seemed a little surprised too. "Our youth leader encourages us to pray and read our Bible every day, so that's how I knew some of the answers. He also says the Holy Spirit helps us when we have a chance to talk about Jesus. And he was right—the words just came to me! Plus, how my friends respond isn't up to me. That's between them and God."

Mason admired his big brother. "So, you read your Bible and learn what you can. You remember God will help you talk to your friends about Jesus. And you don't sweat it because He's the One who helps people understand anyway!"

TODAY'S SPARK

Choose one of the following creative sparks to do today.

1. We follow the Holy Spirit who guides us. Can you follow the pattern below and draw the other half?

2. Use craft sticks to make simple puppets. Draw faces on the sticks, and glue paper clothing on them. With the puppets, act out a conversation between friends about Jesus.

PRAY

God, sometimes I get nervous when talking about Jesus. Help me remember that the other person's response is not up to me. I just want to share Your love. *(Ask God to calm your heart when talking about Him.)*

99

THE HOLY SPIRIT AND GOD'S WORD

No prophecy ever came by the will of man; instead, men spoke from God as they were carried along by the Holy Spirit. *2 Peter 1:21*

Piper always enjoyed it when Pastor Matt visited their Bible study group. Today she had a question for him. "Pastor Matt, we've learned there are sixty-six books in the Bible, written by lots of different people, over hundreds of years. That's a lot of differences. How can we know the Bible is true?"

"Good question, Piper," Pastor Matt said. "And great memory about all of those Bible facts. We call the Bible *God's Word* because God is the ultimate Author of Scripture. He allowed many people to be part of writing and compiling it. But there is a continuous story that weaves all the way through from Genesis to Revelation—it's the story about Jesus!"

Piper thought about this. "If there is a continuous story over sixty-six books written throughout all those years, that seems like something only God could do."

"That's right," said Pastor Matt. "Only God, through the direction of the Holy Spirit, could have given us the Bible."

TODAY'S SPARK

Choose one of the following creative sparks to do today.

1. Plan a way to make study notes in your Bible. You might choose to color code using coloring pencils. Highlight verses you hear during sermons in one color, verses you want to memorize in another, and verses you read during your quiet time in another. Are there any other types of verses you want to highlight?

2. Reread a favorite book, story, or song. Look up the writer and when they lived. Remember that God is the ultimate Author of the Bible.

PRAY

God, Your Word is precious to us. The Bible is unlike any other book in the world! *(Thank God for the Holy Spirit, who helped the authors of the Bible know what to write.)*

100
TRUST HIM

Trust in the LORD with all your heart, and do not rely on your own understanding; in all your ways know him, and he will make your paths straight. *Proverbs 3:5–6*

Wow! You've come to the last devotion in this book. You've studied the Bible and thought about what it said. You've read devotions that helped you think about those Scriptures. You discovered creative ways to study, think, pray, and tell others about Jesus. Way to go!

God has a plan for you. As you read your Bible and think about what it says, the Holy Spirit will help you learn God's truth. Even if you have read a Bible verse before, read it again! You will be surprised how God continues to show you different things if you are faithful to study His Word and pray.

Trust in the Lord with all your heart. Sometimes you won't understand the things happening around you, but don't worry about not understanding. Trust God. Follow His Word, and He promises to guide your path.

TODAY'S SPARK

Choose one of the following creative sparks to do today.

1. What are your favorite ways to be creative? Have you developed any new interests while going through this devotional? Write them in your journal, and list ways you can honor God with that creativity.

2. Draw a large spiral on a piece of paper using a black marker. The lines of the spiral should be an inch or more apart. Begin at the center, and print your name in capital letters so that the top and bottom of each letter touch the lines along the spiral. Repeat printing your name to the end of the spiral. Color the spaces formed using bright colors. Hang your finished art in your room, and remember that God will direct your path.

PRAY

God, help me trust You with all my heart. I want to live an exciting, creative, courageous life with You by the power of Your Holy Spirit! *(Ask God to direct your path so you will always follow His plan for you.)*